UKULELE

Ukulele

The World's
Friendliest Instrument

Daniel Dixon
with Dixie Dixon and Jayne McKay

GIBBS SMITH
TO ENRICH AND INSPIRE HUMANKIND

First Edition
15 14 13 12 11   5 4 3 2 1

Text © 2011 Daniel Dixon
with Dixie Dixon and Jayne McKay
Illustrations © 2011 as noted throughout and on page 144
Photographs © 2011 as noted throughout and on page 144

Published by
Gibbs Smith
P.O. Box 667
Layton, Utah 84041

1.800.835.4993 orders
www.gibbs-smith.com

Designed by Kurt Wahlner
Printed and bound in China
Gibbs Smith books are printed on either recycled, 100%
post-consumer waste, FSC-certified papers or on paper
produced from a 100% certified sustainable forest/
controlled wood source.

Library of Congress Cataloging-in-Publication Data

Dixon, Daniel,
  Ukulele : the world's friendliest instrument / Daniel Dixon
with Dixie Dixon and Jayne McKay. — 1st ed.
     p. cm.
  ISBN 978-1-4236-0369-6
  1. Ukulele. I. Dixon, Dixie. II. McKay, Jayne. III. Title.
  ML1015.U5D59 2011
  787.8'9—dc22
                              2010034832

Contents

Acknowledgments

Thank you to the following people who provided interviews, interest and help of one kind or another: Mike DaSilva, Ian Whitcomb, John Birsner, The Broken G Strings (Beverly Wesley and Georgene Goodwin), Celina Gutierrez, Andy Andrews, Sandor Nagyszalanczy, Peter Thomas, Jim Beloff, and my wife and beloved partner, Dixie.

Daniel Dixon

overture

THE UKULELE has been my very good friend and faithful companion for over sixty years now. It's been a comfort to me when I'm lonely. It's aided me in my courtships. It's supported me in business presentations. It's helped me rejoice and celebrate. It's taught me something about the virtue of humility. And it's always been good for a laugh.

In all this time, my primitive strumming has never really improved. I don't play much better today than I did back then, and I still can't read a note of music or pick out the single-string melody of a simple tune like "Ain't She Sweet?" I just strum and hum along and hope for the best. Ignorance, they say, is bliss.

Or is it?

After decades of mauling my uke in the rudimentary key of C, I began to regret how little I understood its history, its culture and its character. I wanted to know more about my old friend—its past, its present, its future. And so I decided to take George Bernard Shaw's advice. The best way to learn about a subject, he declared, is to write a book about it.

As things turned out, Shaw was dead right. In the writing of my book, I learned more about the ukulele than I ever suspected was there to collect. I already knew, of course, that the uke has been persistently derided as a musical toy of about the same worth as the kazoo or the pennywhistle. I also knew that it was the adopted child of the Hawaiian islanders. The facts are unambiguous. Yet many people, even in Hawaii, continue to believe that the ukulele originated there among the palm-fringed beaches and little grass shacks. Myth and legend have shrouded its ancestry like the mist that rises from Hawaiian waterfalls.

The purpose of this book is not to settle such nettlesome issues. That should be the work of some acknowledged scholar, which I am emphatically not. I am just a man who's come to understand that his ukulele is a truly remarkable instrument. It may have its limitations. It can't summon us to prayer or cause us to weep. It doesn't transfigure or exalt us. But it can almost always make us smile.

This must be the reason why the ukulele is now riding the crest of an international revival. It's more than just a temporary fever—it has all the signs of a permanent movement.

If for any reason you doubt this phenomenon, do yourself a favor. Read no further. Close the book—and also your mind. But if you've started to feel that the ukulele might just be more important than you've ever believed, read on. There are a lot of joys and surprises waiting for you out there in Ukeland.

And who knows? You might just be a part of them.

FROM PORTUGaL to Paradise

The Uke Goes Hawaiian: 1879-1915

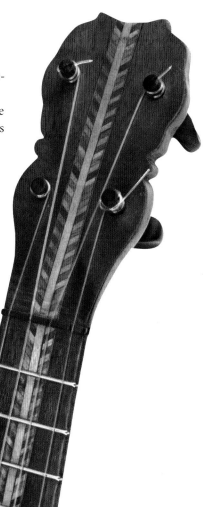

THE ORIGINS of the ukulele are as uncertain as an alley cat's.

Nobody knows for sure when, where or by whom the uke was first created. In Greece? In Spain? The authorities differ, and sometimes bicker.

On this conclusion, though, even the cantankerous scholars agree. The parents of the ukulele were clearly Europeans, not Polynesians. The experts also concur that at some obscure date the ukulele migrated to Portugal.

They didn't call it a ukulele in those days. That came later. The Portuguese defined it as a *machete,* or sometimes as a *machimbo* or a *machim* or a *braquinho.* It didn't take the machete long to become a respected musical citizen of Portugal. Especially on the Portuguese island of Madeira, it was a regular guest at fiestas and dances and weddings—wherever people gathered to have a good time.

It also traveled, usually on ships. Some of these journeys took it a long, long way from home.

The Portuguese of that era were acknowledged to be the world's master mariners, and the machetes they carried with them must have been a great comfort to these seamen. Music provided recreation and helped relieve the monotony of voyages that seemed to never end.

Some of these Portuguese vessels dropped anchor in the harbors the Atlantic had carved from the coast of Brazil. The crews swarmed ashore to satisfy their lusts and their longings. And just to help out with the singing and the dancing, they took along their machetes.

But these men were more than just mariners; they were also conquerors and colonists. And they had some serious business to pursue there in Brazil.

Like the Portuguese settlements they helped to establish, their diminutive four-string instrument soon blended into the Brazilian landscape. The natives took to it as enthusiastically as they did to other European refinements of dress and deportment. They gave it a name of their own—the *cavaco*. And with the cavaco they played a hip-twitching music of their own—the samba, the cholo. In Brazil today, many bands and orchestras reserve a special place for the guy who plays the cavaco.

Over the next hundred years or so, the wind went out of the Portuguese sails. Its dreams of glory and empire faded. By the nineteenth century the kingdom was becalmed and drifting toward political and economic insignificance.

On Madeira, despite the hard times, the machete continued to thrive. The people who made and played them, however, did not. They began to immigrate, headed for wherever work and opportunity could be found.

On August 23rd, 1879, after rounding the Horn, steaming up the coast of South America and then across the Pacific, the British ship *Ravenscrag* finally reached the port of Honolulu.

Its journey from Madeira to Hawaii had taken four months and covered fifteen thousand miles. The ship was crowded with 423 Portuguese fugitives from poverty. Most of the men had contracted to work on the Hawaiian sugar plantations for about ten dollars per month. The languorous Hawaiians didn't find that kind of sweat-stained labor congenial. Their climate was gentle. The sea seethed with

easily netted fish. The trees drooped with succulent tropical fruit. Let the immigrants swing those picks and chop that sugarcane.

The *Ravenscrag*'s arrival didn't cause the islanders to ignite any fireworks. They'd been watching such visitors come and go for 150 years. The first to appear were the Spanish galleons and the British men-of-war, then came the American whalers, and after that the traders and merchant vessels. Their holds were crammed with goods and merchandise of every kind, but especially with anything made of iron and steel—hardware, tools, utensils, stoves, machinery, railroad tracks and locomotives.

These cargoes certainly fueled progress, but not all of them were entirely benign. Often they included cutthroat speculators out to make the quickest dollar they could swindle. Missionaries were also

unloaded on the islanders—zealots who sought to supplant the ancient Hawaiian gods and ceremonies with threats of fire and brimstone. They brought diseases, too—syphilis, smallpox, cholera. No introduction of leprosy was necessary. Hawaii was already well acquainted with that appalling malady.

What happened when the *Ravenscrag* docked in Hawaii has been described by some chroniclers with transports of imagination. "In celebration of their arrival," one of them writes, "João Fernandes borrowed his friend's braquinho, jumped out of the ship, and started playing songs from his native land on the wharf. The Hawaiians who came down to the dock were very impressed by the speed of this musician's fingers as they danced across the fingerboard, and they called the instrument 'ukulele,' which translates into English as 'jumping flea.'

You see, that was the image conjured up by those flying fingers."

Well, it's a pretty little story, but it's probably just a fairy tale. Certainly nobody on that wharf ever invoked the word "ukulele." Several years would pass before the term was ever invented.

Much more credible is the article published in the *Hawaiian Gazette* a couple of weeks later. "Madeira Islanders recently arrived here," it reported, "have been delighting the people with nightly street concerts." The piece goes on to state that the performers played "strange instruments which are kind of a cross between a guitar and a banjo."

Those instruments didn't remain strange to the islanders for very long. As soon as they'd worked off their contracts to the sugar plantations, three accomplished cabinetmakers opened their own shops in Honolulu. Their names were Manuel Nunes, Augusto Dias and José do Espirito Santo. Two were adept musicians. They made furniture but also crafted and repaired guitars, along with other Portuguese stringed instruments that were starting to circulate under yet another name—"taro patch fiddles."

All of these craftsmen began to advertise their wares in the middle of the 1880s. The machete soon began to catch on. But it was still basically a Portuguese, rather than a Hawaiian, instrument. And then it got the best and biggest boost it could have been accorded: it was accepted as a royal Hawaiian instrument.

King David Kalakaua was probably a more dedicated musician than he was a monarch. He was proficient on the guitar, the mandolin, the accordion and the piano, and he was also a talented composer. King Kalakaua's power to govern was already limping to an end, and he would be forced to surrender most of his power to the United States in 1887. By 1890, his life began limping to an end, and he died in San

⬆ Music buff King David Kalakaua

The experiment became a love affair. He ordered the royal composers to feature it in the scores and arrangements that supported the liquid movements of the hula dancers.

It was then and there in the royal palace that the machete may finally have become the "ukulele." Exactly when and how this occurred nobody really knows. One theory involves a shadowy and sinister character named Edward Purvis. He was a young English army officer who somehow insinuated himself into the palace and wrangled an appointment as the king's assistant chamberlain.

Purvis was small, slight and fidgety. His nervous energy inspired a nickname: "Ukulele," which, as mentioned earlier, means "jumping flea" in Hawaiian. He turned out to be the Iago of King Kalakaua's court. He was charged by the prime minister, Walter Murray Gibson, of treacherous intrigues against the king. One eminent scholar notes: "Gibson suspected Purvis was passing unflattering information to the king's opponents, and that he was the author of two notorious pamphlets published anonymously, that portrayed Kalakaua as a drunken, womanizing aboriginal dunce, and the son of a Negro menial with no claim to the crown."

At least in some respects that lurid description seems accurate. Robert Louis Stevenson wrote to a friend about the king's almost infinite capacity for champagne. "A bottle of fizz," Stevenson reported. "It's like a glass of sherry to him; he thinks nothing of five or six bottles in an afternoon as a whet for dinner." And early Portuguese virtuoso João Fernandes later recalled: "We would go to the king's

Francisco in 1891. His sister, Princess Lili'uokalani, inherited what was left of the throne as queen.

The extravagance of Kalakaua's court, however, was never restrained by ominous signs of collapse. He continued to act as a patron of the arts and to offer his palace as a theater for dance and music recitals. One of the three Portuguese machete makers, immigrant Augusto Dias, was regularly retained to play at the king's soirées and poker parties. Robert Louis Stevenson was among the notables who frequently dropped by the palace to join the festivities and share in the fun. He occasionally toodled his flageolet, a cousin of the recorder, accompanied by Dias on the machete.

At some point during this period the King himself began to study the machete.

bungalow. The king wouldn't stay in the palace—just when there was business. Lots of people came. Plenty kanakas. Much music, much hula, much kaukau, much drink. All time plenty drink. And King Kalakaua, he pay for all!"

Though Purvis may have been telling the truth, he had clearly been disloyal. The king was outraged. He considered it treachery more odious than any other crime. When he investigated, he concluded that the prime minister had indeed been right to blow the whistle on his assistant chamberlain. Purvis was banished to the United States, where he died two years later.

A second speculation about the evolution of the term "ukulele" centers on Queen Lili'uokalani. She was an aristocrat with a fastidious distaste for the unseemly. To call this cherished little instrument a "jumping flea" was, the queen felt, inelegant and boorish.

Then research revealed that "ukulele," like many Hawaiian words, had another meaning. It could also be poetically interpreted as "the gift that comes." This was the reading that the queen passionately preferred. Her resistance melted. Soon the issue was no longer being debated. Inside the palace and out, what had once been known as the machete was now the ukulele.

THERE'S NO QUESTION that its royal patrons enhanced the public's awareness and appreciation of the machete. But in the end, it probably didn't become the ukulele because of majestic influence. That shift was decided by economics.

At first the makers had marketed their machetes chiefly to the Portuguese community, which naturally responded to a name that evoked memories of their homeland. The islanders, though, felt no such sentimental attachment. To attract their very considerable business, it was imperative to give the instrument a name that sounded Hawaiian. "Ukulele" did exactly that, eventually with very gratifying results.

The royal favor had lit a fire under the ukulele. But it was a modest blaze at first, not an immediate conflagration. It took time to spread and intensify. That was partly because it also took a lot of time to handcraft a ukulele of superior quality. The process was laborious, arduous and exacting.

The premier Hawaiian ukuleles were and are shaped from the wood of the native koa. These trees grow chiefly in the high mountains on the island of Hawaii. The tree's color is an exquisite blend of red and brown, and its grain is ideal for the tools of the craftsmen. Back in the 1880s, it could take weeks simply to identify the most promising candidates. Then the selected trees had to be harvested, hauled and shipped to Honolulu, where they were milled into lumber and seasoned until they were ready for the saw, the plane, the chisel and the knife. Now, finally,

◑ **Hawaiian Queen Lili'uokalani**

the very few Hawaiian artisans adequately skilled for work of this kind could go to their benches.

In his admirable visual history of the ukulele, Jim Beloff quotes from an article published in 1946 by Augusto Dias's granddaughter Elma Cabral describing how Dias approached his formidable task.

"Grandpa sawed koa into thin strips and wrapped them around a mold he had prepared. Gluing the edges, he tied cord around it to keep it in shape. Then he chiseled out an 'arm' that was to be glued to the main body. On this arm he made grooves, which were inlaid with strips of metal forming the musical scale. He drilled four holes on one end of the arm. Then he whittled four pegs to fit tightly into these holes. He cut thin strips of contrasting wood on the bias, gluing them around the edge of the instrument and around the large opening where the sound escaped. This was created so skillfully that the joining of the strips could not be detected by the human eye. He sanded the instrument to a satiny finish before he applied varnish. Cat-gut strings were knotted and attached to slots in the pegs and to raised pieces of wood on the opposite end of the instrument. After testing the scale and strumming a few chords to test the tone, Grandpa applied his seal on the inside of the instrument."

This routine was faithfully repeated, step by step, with every instrument Dias created. As a result, his production figures remained a trickle and demand continued to exceed supply. Nobody was getting rich on these exertions, either. In those very different days, you could buy a handcrafted ukulele for as little as $3, though elite editions embellished with ornate mother-of-pearl inlays could run all the way up to $35

☙ Queen Lili'uokalani was as musically
  gifted as her brother. She penned
  the music and lyrics to the legendary
  Hawaiian song "Aloha Oe."

(around $400 in today's dollars). Money back then, like promises, was worth a lot more than it is today.

By about 1890, however, the immigrant guitar and ukulele makers had managed to develop a more skillful and sufficient workforce. Business began to quicken. Sales multiplied, especially after the makers started to advertise their instruments in English-speaking journals and newspapers.

Manuel Nunes was perhaps the most enterprising of the three Portuguese competitors. He was one of the first to promote the "ukulele" in print. One of his advertisements cited the patronage of the royal family, and he also proclaimed himself to be the ukulele's inventor. The assertion was a brazen whopper, but Nunes persistently repeated the same false claim for years to come.

From their richly paneled offices, astute and powerful businessmen watched these developments with intense interest. They'd conspired to help topple the feeble Hawaiian Royal monarchy in 1893, and now they were poised to exploit the expected advantages. In the ukulele phenomenon they sniffed opportunity as the fox smells dinner in the hen house. So they sat down to figure out a marketing scheme.

Now that the ukulele had become so popular in Hawaii, they reasoned, maybe it could serve as a symbol of the islands. Maybe it could suggest their lure, their legends, their easygoing ways. Maybe it could help induce American travelers to book passage on their ocean liners and to lodge in their hotels and dine at their ritzy restaurants and buy their flamboyant Hawaiian shirts and muumuus.

In other words—maybe they could export the Hawaiian ukulele and import a whole lot of money.

Anyway, the businessmen thought the idea was worth a try.

What happened next is quite a story.

Get your Congressmen
TO VOTE FOR THE
PANAMA-PACIFIC
INTERNATIONAL EXPOSITION
AT THE EXPOSITION CITY
SAN FRANCISCO-1915
CALIFORNIA GUARANTEES AN EXPOSITION
THAT WILL BE A CREDIT
TO THE NATION

The Panama-Pacific International Expo showed Hawaii—and the exotic ukulele—to the world.

california, here i come

Mania on the Mainland: 1915-1920

TO THE UKULELE PIONEERS who arrived from Hawaii in the early 1900s, the United States was an unexplored frontier. The instrument they strummed was an eccentric novelty to most Americans. So was the sound and style of their music. It possessed a lilt and a languor that just about nobody on the mainland had ever heard. It was music that seemed hedonistic, intended to stimulate nothing more or less than pure pleasure. One newspaper reviewer described it as "weirdly sensuous."

Exactly how much support these performers received from U.S. business tycoons is anybody's guess. The details are murky, though one fact seems indisputably clear. The musicians were dispatched by their

☉ A Manuel Nunes uke from the very early days.

sponsors from Hawaii with blessings more material than a chorus of alohas. They journeyed from engagement to engagement in what was obviously an organized campaign.

Until about 1910 a few scattered Hawaiian groups toured the Eastern states in traveling tent shows, then more elegantly known as "chautauquas." They also worked the prevailing vaudeville circuits, usually as supporting acts for the headliners. They shuffled off to Buffalo for an extended appearance at a world's fair, journeyed west to Omaha for another, and then ventured to Portland and Seattle for two more. The response was polite but reserved. No mobs of adoring fans swarmed over the performers. There at the start, it was a tough struggle.

In Chicago, for instance, the ukulele and Hawaiian music were featured for the first time on the legitimate stage. The cast of one hundred included damsels who billed themselves as "Rose Dolly" and "Flossy Hope." The title of the play—*The Echo*—was nothing short of prophetic. An echo is what it soon became. Audiences avoided it in droves. It ignominiously closed after a brief run, but out in Los Angeles, another impresario was waiting impatiently in the wings. His name was Oliver Morosco, and he was undaunted by any obituaries that had been written about *The Echo*. Like most successful producers, he possessed the gift of confidence. His enthusiasm was contagious. From one of the hardnosed businessmen who helped to dethrone King Kalakaua, he raised the money he needed to stage a lurid melodrama called *The Bird of Paradise*.

Set among the throbbing drums and lush vegetation of Hawaii, the play had all the ingredients of a Victorian tear- or fearjerker—the sinister missionary, the rapacious sugar baron, the innocent and trusting tribesmen, the doomed and valiant lovers. He was a

🔊 This sheet music from Bird of Paradise depicts Hawaiian maiden Luana, presumably before she is sacrificed to the gods.

heroic young American, she a Hawaiian princess. Her gods, she knew, were angered by their romance. Only by the sacrifice of her life, only by casting herself into the fiery crater of the sacred volcano, could she

five talented musicians from the islands to supply this enhancement. They called themselves, with a drab lack of imagination, the "Hawaiian Quintette," but they turned out to be the life of the party. Two of the group's five members played the ukulele, an instrument most of the audience had never seen or heard before. Their strummings and pluckings sharpened every menace, heightened every entreaty, intensified every embrace. Ah, those quaint little ukuleles! They just about stole the show.

With the critics, *The Bird of Paradise* laid something of an egg. But after a rather sluggish start, that egg proved to be golden. Once it hit the road, it became a box-office bonanza. In its highly successful New York run, a young actress named Laurette Taylor stared in the role of the martyred princess. She also essayed a suggestive but entirely inaccurate version of the hula, intended to arouse rather than educate the audience. This was the same Laurette Taylor who later became one of the most honored actresses of the American stage.

From New York, *The Bird of Paradise* winged its way all across the United States, up into Canada, over to England, making a mint of money at every engagement. Wherever it went, the ukulele went too. Every performance was to some extent an advertisement for this novel little instrument. But the big breakthrough came later, when the Panama Pacific International Exposition opened for business in 1915.

THE NOBLE PURPOSE of the exposition was to celebrate, at last, the completion of the Panama Canal.

That was something to cheer about, all right. But San Francisco had another motive as well. Nine years had passed since it had been devastated by the earthquake of 1906. In that interval, the city had

appease their wrath and save her beloved. Farewell, cruel world!

If all this hokum wasn't enough to satisfy the audience, there was still another excitement that brought them to the edge of their seats. It was the music—the *Hawaiian* music—that accompanied the whole bizarre performance. Morosco had imported re-created itself. It was a superb display of courage, determination and bravado. That was worth a celebration too. Three years before the ditch in Panama finally became a canal that linked the two oceans, San Francisco began to plan a joint jubilee.

The courts, the pavilions, the temples, the gardens, the fountains, the bazaars—all of them looked as though they might last forever. In fact, they were intended to be easily and quickly destroyed. San Francisco real estate was even then too valuable to lodge the derelict fossils of a bygone exposition. Today only one relic remains—a Palace of Fine Arts that has since served as a museum, a warehouse and a garage.

Snuggled away amid this maze of grandeur was a transported island of Hawaii. The mission of this exhibit was to acquaint tourists with the seductions that awaited them out there across the blue Pacific. The pleasures included music performed on ukuleles. A cluster of Hawaiian musicians strummed and harmonized to the visitors from exhibit to exhibit. Their defining number was "On the Beach at Waikiki." Both the song and the Hawaiian gardens became a sensation. "The canaries have heard the music so often," one cynical journalist noted, "that at certain times they take up the tune and sing the accompaniment." Another writer stated that the Hawaiian concession stand peddled "thousands of ukuleles to tourists who returned to their hometowns with their exotic instruments and visions of island paradise in their heads."

It's certainly possible that many visitors were intoxicated by what they saw and heard there at the Hawaiian gardens, but to claim that thousands of them ever purchased ukuleles is clearly a bloated exaggeration. The ukulele trade in 1915 was still controlled by a few Portuguese makers in Hawaii. Their shops were small and their handcrafted output remained meager. No techniques of mass ukulele production had yet been developed, and only one Hawaiian maker, Jonah Kumalae, operated anything like a real factory. He's said to have turned out three hundred ukes a month, though this too is probably an inflated figure. It would have required a team of at least twelve specialists—more than any single proprietor would have been able to hire in Hawaii at that time. Besides, Kumalae was a notably proud and painstaking man. He refused to rush any instrument to market before it was as good as he could make it. At the exposition, where he occupied a special booth, the Kumalae ukuleles were honored with a coveted gold medal for excellence.

Despite the limited supply of merchandise for sale, the exposition kindled an unprecedented ukulele craze. The infatuation swept up and down the Pacific Coast, then surged out across the country. Often it followed the road companies of *The Bird of*

↰ ↱ A very nice example of a ukulele made by Jonah Kumalae. Placed in the strings is a picture of David Bourne, a saloon player and the original owner of this ukulele.

↑ ➔ The back and front of yet another Manuel Nunes ukulele from the early days.

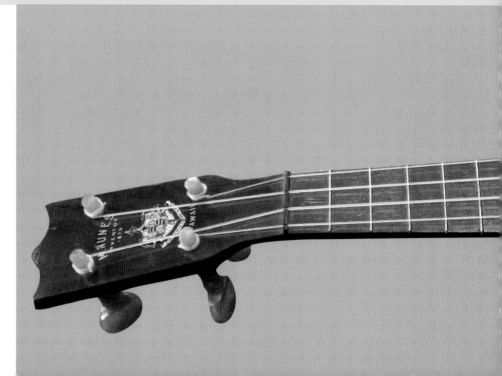

Paradise, which was drawing full houses all over the landscape. Wherever it played, the craze was pretty sure to follow. And as it spread, the demand for ukes became more and more insistent. The scope and urgency of this hunger triggered an immediate response both on the mainland and in the islands. On the ocean liners, stewards now strummed the ukulele when they weren't serving drinks or setting up deck chairs. Hawaiian uke virtuosos began to surface too. Prodigies like Ernest Kaai had been around for some time, but now they came off the beaches and away from the luaus to entertain for serious money in the mansions and elite hotels. Kaai was among the first ukists to be featured in the fashionable Hawaiian orchestras. He also authored two early books of ukulele instruction, one in 1906 and the other in 1916. The second volume—*The Ukulele, the Hawaiian Guitar*—is more sophisticated than its predecessor, which is basically a manual for beginners. He treats the ukulele with profound and passionate respect, demonstrates the mastery of advanced chords and intricate fingerings, and argues that it affords a player more pleasure per month than can be derived "from any stringed instrument in a year."

Meantime, the Hawaiian makers were gearing up for the ukulele boom. Three of them led the pack. The first was Jonah Kumalae, just back

The Kamaka ukulele benefited from former Nunes employee Sam Kamaka's determination to strike out on his own, thereby adding output for the uke craze of the 1910s and '20s.

A fine example of the ukulele craze in California is demonstrated by these five lovelies strumming away in Santa Monica.

from his triumph from the Pan-Pacific Exposition in San Francisco. The second was Manuel Nunes, who shamelessly described himself as "the inventor of the ukulele." Together with his sons, Nunes continued to produce exceptional ukes until the business finally went belly up in 1935, a victim of hard times and changing tastes. The third leader was Samuel Kamaka, once an apprentice of Nunes. He left in 1916 to establish his own shop in the cramped, dark basement of his house. Ninety-two years later, the enterprise is still going strong. It's now known as Kamaka Hawaii Incorporated—the only line of Hawaiian ukuleles to survive as a brand name from that day to this.

As the islanders were equipping themselves for bonanza business, eager mainland makers were also getting into the act. At its height, the ukulele craze affected every part of the nation. Cities, towns, villages, even farms and ranches—none of them was left unaddled. But nowhere did the fever descend with more vehement force, and nowhere was it more skillfully cultivated for profit, than in a nest of dingy New York offices called Tin Pan Alley.

Q Another fine example of a vintage Kamaka Pineapple Ukulele.

give my Regards to Broadway

The Uke, Tin Pan Alley and the Roaring Twenties

NOBODY REALLY KNOWS how, why or when Tin Pan Alley acquired its name. One fact, however, is certain. It was never an actual alley or even a specific street address. Like Hell's Kitchen or the Bowery, it designated a sort of neighborhood.

The original site seems to have been a cluster of offices that border Union Square at East Fourteenth Street in Manhattan. That was somewhere around 1900. By 1914 it had moved uptown to West Twenty-Eighth Street between Broadway and Fifth Avenue, twelve blocks closer to the Theatre District.

But Tin Pan Alley was more than just a location. It was also a culture.

The tenants who occupied those shabby, crowded five-story buildings were almost all connected with show business. They had their own customs and beliefs, their own heroes and villains, their own codes of conduct. They were producers, publishers, talent agents, performers, publicists and musicians. And, of course, they

☾ ☽ Much of the sheet music from Tin Pan Alley included arrangements for the oh-so-popular ukulele.

🔊 Tin Pan Alley was home to composers and songwriters such as these heavy hitters. From left to right: Gene Buck, Victor Herbert, John Philip Sousa, Harry B. Smith, Jerome Kern, Irving Berlin, George W. Meyer, Irving Bibo, and Otto Harbach.

were songwriters—the most raucous, sentimental, irreverent, clever and gifted brotherhood of tunesmiths in the world.

Between the turn of the century and the middle 1930s, songs poured out of Tin Pan Alley like water over Niagara Falls. Many were romantic ballads that explored every possible rhyme with moon—croon, June, spoon, tune, soon, boon. Others were quirky novelties like "Yes! We Have No Bananas," and "If I Give Up the Saxophone (Will You Come Back to

Me?)" Still others were musical responses to whatever happened to be in vogue or in the headlines at the time—the first World War ("Over There" and "Hello Central, Give Me No Man's Land"), hotly debated social and political issues ("Evolution Mama, Don't You Make a Monkey Out of Me"), the latest dance craze ("Charleston" and "Cake-Walkin' Babies From Home"), and even the most popular comic strips of the era ("Barney Google, With His Goo-Goo-Googly Eyes"). The residents of Tin Pan Alley could

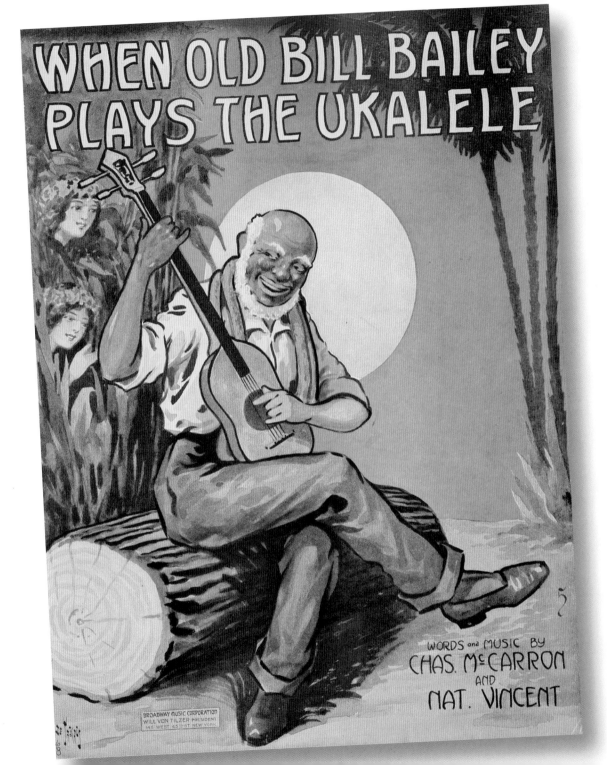

create, publish and circulate a song on almost any event or occasion, and almost overnight. Just days after Charles Lindbergh flew for the first time across the Atlantic, a song called "Lucky Lindy" was being peddled at the music stores. It sold like hot dogs at the World Series.

In the early days, a songwriter's income was derived from the sales of sheet music. At first the tunes were scored almost exclusively for the piano. But when the country broke out in a serious case of ukephoria, Tin Pan Alley was quick to react. Popular sheet music began to offer an additional chart-ing of chords for the uke. Soon every song that seemed remotely plausible was scored both for the piano and the ukulele.

This was the decisive develop-ment that turned the ukulele from a temporary seizure into a national addic-tion. Sheet music carried the virus into millions of Americans' homes. The uke might not be as refined as the piano, but it was a whole lot easier to play, a whole lot less expensive, and a whole lot more por-table. You couldn't take a piano along on a picnic or (as the song goes) while "Paddlin' Madeleine Home" in a canoe.

It's regrettable that Irving Berlin, who wrote an astounding three thousand songs over his long and brilliant career, never composed one about the ukulele. But plenty of his fellow tunesmiths found the subject right up their Tin Pan Alley. The first offering—an obscure relic called "When Old Bill Bailey Plays the Ukalele"—appeared in 1915 at about the same time the Pan-Pacific International Exposition opened in San Francisco. It was followed by another, and then another, and after that, throughout the Roaring Twenties, by perhaps a couple of dozen more. Here are just some of their titles:

"My Waikiki Ukulele Girl"
"I Could Hear the Ukuleles Calling Me"
"That Ukalele Band"
"When They Play the Rosary on the Ukulele"
"My Honolulu Ukulele Baby"
"Ukulele Blues"
"Give Me a Ukulele (and a Ukulele Baby) and Leave the Rest to Me"
"Say It with a Ukulele"
"Under the Ukulele Tree"

YAAKA HULA HICKEY DULA

(HAWAIIAN LOVE SONG)

BY
E. RAY GOETZ
JOE YOUNG &
PETE WENDLING

Successfully Introduced by
AL JOLSON in
ROBINSON CRUSOE, JR.
At The Winter Garden
NEW YORK.

ukist, employed different tools and techniques. Songs like "Hum and Strum" and "They're Wearin' 'Em Higher in Hawaii" suggested the presence of a uke in the cover art of sheet music, or in evocative language, or in a combination of both. "Yaaka Hula Hickey Dula," for instance, could only have been a tribute to Hawaii—and to the ukulele.

The most enduring (and maybe the most endearing) ukulele song ever written was published in 1925. The words were the work of Gus Kahn, who also supplied the lyrics for such Tin Pan Alley immortals as "I'll See You in My Dreams" and "It Had to Be You." The title was "Ukulele Lady," and this is how it begins.

"If you – like – a ukulele lady,
Ukulele lady like-a you;
If you – like – to linger
where it's shady,
Ukulele lady linger too."

What happens after that is ambiguous. The listener is left to imagine the erotic consequences, but they were sufficiently vivid to make the song an instant hit.

Meantime, over in the islands, native songwriters picked up the beat and joined the party. One of them was Harry Owens, who later composed "Sweet Leilani" and became the musical director of a radio show that was beamed to the mainland and was enticingly titled *Hawaii Calls*. The islands made their contributions to the ukulele craze, but they never mounted a serious challenge to the mainland

"Ukulele Lou"
"Oh, How She Could Play the Ukulele"
"On My Ukulele"

The best way to sell a ukulele song to the intended market was to include the name of the instrument in the title. All of the tunes just noted do exactly that. Many others, though, also aiming at the dedicated

tunesmiths. Compared to Tin Pan Alley, songwriting in Hawaii was almost a dead end.

The ukulele craze probably couldn't have happened without the aid of sheet music but it was also powered by two other sources as well.

One was the phenomenon called radio. Electricity had already wired most of the country for light. Now it was also wired for sound. Any household that could afford it, and some that couldn't, had acquired a set of some kind. Many were lodged in massive

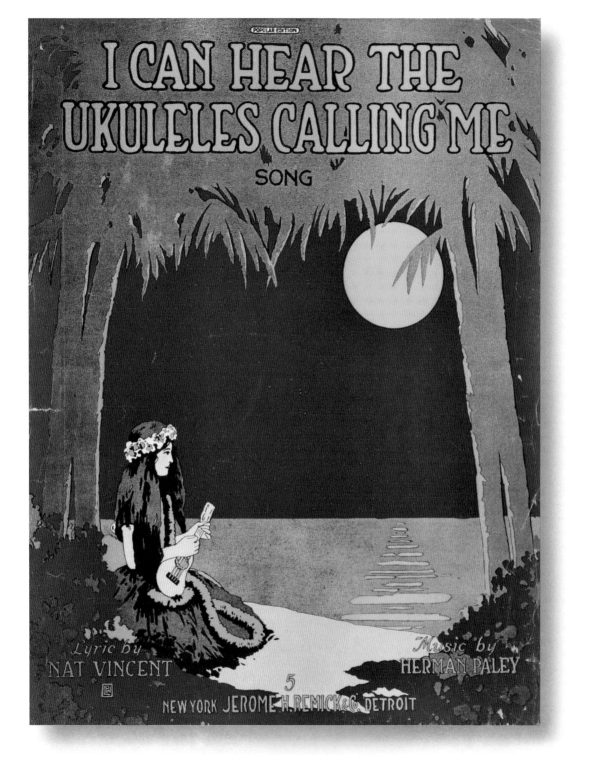

consoles that dominated the front parlors and living rooms of families, who gathered to tune in to their favorite programs. Many of these shows were aired by new national networks, but even more were produced by hundreds of local stations that were scattered all across the country. Most towns of any size possessed some kind of broadcasting capability, often located in a run-down building out at the edge of city limits.

Then, as now, music was an essential part of the radio business. It helped sell three very different but related products—instruments, records and hand-cranked Victrolas. The songwriters flourished. The manufacturers prospered. And some of the performers—players, singers, personalities—stepped into the spotlight. Suddenly, and often surprisingly, they became stars.

Cliff
edwards,
"ukulele
ike"

The music goes 'Round and 'Round

The Great Early Players

OF ALL THE AMERICAN ukists who were destined for stardom, Cliff Edwards probably tops the list. He was born in Mark Twain's hometown of Hannibal, Missouri, and was out on his own before he started to shave. A jaunty man with the huge dark eyes of a raccoon and a sweet pure voice that could span three octaves, he made his way to St. Louis, where he laboriously taught himself to play the uke. Like most of his uke-playing contemporaries, he found himself wanting an easy-to-carry, easy-to-play instrument to tote around to bars (which might or might not have had a piano and accompanist). For a struggling performer, the uke was an inexpensive, accessible choice. Edwards sang in saloons for nickels and dimes, and there he picked up the nickname "Ukulele Ike." For the next couple of years, he toured with various carnivals and tent shows, just barely managing to get by.

About the end of World War I, Edwards landed in Chicago and made a name for himself in vaudeville. His skills as a

↩ Native Missourian Cliff Edwards left home as a kid, learned the ukulele, became a saloon singer, became "Ukulele Ike," and before long, was in Hollywood, introducing the song "Singin' in the Rain" to the world and becoming the voice of Jiminy Cricket for Walt Disney's film Pinocchio.

↪ Cliff Edwards and his wife.

43

character actor and his warm, melodious voice gave him instant appeal on the stage.

First with an already renowned vaudeville headliner, a stuttering comedian named Joe Frisco, then with other partners, often as a solo act, Edwards remained a star in vaudeville until the talkies put it out of business in the 1930s. Meantime, he was kept very busy in the recording studios. He signed a deal with a Pathé label in 1923, and over the next decade he produced hundreds of titles in dozens of sessions. Sometimes he was accompanied by sidemen—groups like Fred Ozark's Jug Blowers or Andy Ioana and His Islanders. Now and then he shared recording dates with such noted jazzmen as cornetist Red Nichols and trombone whiz Miff Mole.

More often than not, though, the recordings featured just Edwards and his Martin ukulele. That was all he ever needed to put over a song, no matter what kind of song it happened to be. He tackled material of every description—old songs, new songs, novelty tunes, the complete menu. Some of the selections were rankly suggestive—barnyard humor set to music—and others may have been too sweetly sentimental, but there was one failing he never committed. It's been estimated that over seventy million Cliff Edwards records were sold over the course of his career, and not one of them was ever pompous or pretentious.

Once he'd managed to stand vaudeville on its ear, Edwards developed another specialty. The producers of lavish Broadway musicals began casting him in roles designed to introduce certain songs of special importance. When George Gershwin's *Lady, Be Good* opened in 1924, in was Ukulele Ike who first told the world about "Fascinatin' Rhythm." He did, however, get some help from Fred and Adele Astaire, who danced up a storm as Edwards sang and strummed his ukulele. "The callous Broadwayites cheered them," wrote one reviewer, "as if their favorite halfback had planted the ball behind the goalpost after an eighty-yard run."

Edwards adroitly juggled many such assignments throughout the Roaring Twenties. Several of the songs he introduced and promoted later became standards and are still performed today. Curiously, one that didn't was a number buried in an early MGM musical called *Hollywood Revue of 1929*. The producer, Irving Thalberg, had signed Edwards to appear in a series of MGM short subjects, but when the full-length feature went into production he was hired to work his introductory magic on a composition called "Singin' in the Rain." Neither the song nor the film excited much response at the time. Not until twenty-five years later did "Singin' in the Rain" become the title of a smash hit that Pauline Kael, the *New Yorker*'s feared and formidable movie critic, pronounced "the best Hollywood musical ever made."

By now Edwards was based in Los Angeles. Over the next couple of years he worked in thirty-three MGM productions, sometimes as a musician, sometimes as an actor, sometimes both. These days he is best known as the voice of Jiminy Cricket in Walt Disney's *Pinocchio*. The studio was then seeking a unique voice for the character, who was also slated to sing the picture's signature song, "When You Wish Upon a Star." Edwards was the thirty-seventh candidate tested for the part. When he turned out to be the voice of Jiminy Cricket, "When You Wish Upon a Star" became his as well. He owned the song in the same way that Judy Garland owned "Over the Rainbow."

Though the rest of Edwards' story is not a happy one—his career slowly faded, he spent too much, drank too much, and ended up dying penniless and alone (the Disney company paid for his simple gravestone)—"Ukulele Ike" remains firmly a part of pop culture history.

WHO TAKES CARE
OF THE
CARETAKER'S DAUGHTER
(While The Caretaker's Busy Taking Care)

by Chick Endor

with Ukelele Arrangement.

Introduced by
**CLIFF
EDWARDS**
(Ukelele Ike)

In The
Successful Musical
Comedy

LADY, BE GOOD

at The
Liberty Theatre
New York

ILLUSTRATED SELF-TEACHING METHOD

HOW TO PLAY
UKULELE

THE

Roy Smeck

WAY

You can quickly learn to play the Ukulele by using the Roy Smeck easy-to-follow diagrams. No music training is necessary. Learn how to strum the strings in a few self-taught lessons. Tuning made easy. Learn songs everyone loves.

ROY SMECK
Wizard of the Strings
Star of Stage, Screen, Radio-
Television and Recording Artist

PRICE
75¢

PUBLISHED BY **HARRY VOLPE** 115 WEST 48th STREET, NEW YORK CITY

ROY SMECK

EVEN AT THE SUMMIT of his popularity, Edwards had his challengers. The most redoubtable was Roy Smeck, perhaps the most amazing technician ever to make the ukulele yield its hidden charms.

From the day that he first picked up a musical instrument, Smeck never wanted to do anything else. As a kid, he almost practiced himself into a nervous breakdown. Once he decided to concentrate on banjo, guitar, harmonica and the ukulele, he steadied and settled down. He was still in his teens when he hit the vaudeville circuit.

Smeck couldn't sing. And music alone, no matter how artfully rendered, wasn't enough to satisfy the vaudeville audience. So Smeck developed a novelty act. He'd strum the banjo or the ukulele and, at the same time, tooted the harmonica. He played the uke behind his back, plucked its strings with his teeth, bowed its strings as he might a violin. His range of tricks and techniques was amazing; he even learned how to create the staccato of tap dancing on the body of the uke. He became a musical acrobat, a contortionist. The audience didn't just sigh in wonder at what he did. They also gasped in surprise.

Smeck was a master of the guitar, the banjo and the harmonica, but the ukulele was his abiding passion. He ardently explored all its possibilities and in time was recognized as an authentic virtuoso. He was invited to perform at Franklin D. Roosevelt's first presidential inauguration in 1932 and later played at the coronation of King George VI in 1936. He toured the United States and the world, one triumph after another. Not bad for a kid from the coal-dusted town of Reading, Pennsylvania.

Like Ukulele Ike, Smeck appeared in several pioneer film shorts. They helped establish him as a celebrity—the "Wizard of the Strings." He was almost as active in the recording studios as Edwards. Archivists have tracked down five hundred sides and seventeen different Smeck albums. On some he plays banjo and guitar, on others only the ukulele. The selections were drawn from all over the musical universe, including America, Hawaii and Europe. Folk classics, sentimental ballads, popular favorites, Viennese waltzes, even rousing marches like "The Stars and Stripes Forever"—Smeck could transfigure almost anything scored for strings.

Smeck considered himself as much a teacher as he did a performer. Over his career, he authored over thirty songbooks and instruction manuals. When he went on the road, he often conducted classes and seminars for both beginners and advanced students. He even designed his own pear-shaped incarnation of the ukulele—the Vita-Uke. Millions were sold. It was just one of several lines marketed under his name by the Harmony Company of Chicago.

Q The great ukulele virtuosos of the '20s, '30s, and '40s became ambassadors for the instrument. Roy Smeck wrote instruction books and the Harmony Company asked him to design his own ukulele, the Vita-Uke.

richard konter

ONE OF the most remarkable ukaholics of the Roaring Twenties was not a professional entertainer at all. Richard Konter was an explorer, and his era was the Freezing Twenties. A member of Admiral Byrd's first expedition to reach the Pole, he carried his uke into the Arctic wastes along with other essential supplies and equipment. Konter, it seems, was just as determined to acquaint the Inuit with the noble ukulele as he was to plant the American flag at the intended goal.

As it turned out, no Eskimos existed in those ice-bound latitudes. It was too cold for them. But Konter's cherished Martin ukulele, crafted from Hawaiian koa wood, made it to the North Pole. The entire company signed it, including the frosty Admiral Richard Byrd. In his indispensable *Visual History of the Ukulele*, Jim Beloff describes his reception when the expedition came home to the United States. "Konter was met in New York by twenty young women, who were former ukulele students, playing ukes in honor of his return. Later on, Konter gave the plain (but signed) little uke to the Martin Company and today it can be found in the Martin Museum in Nazareth, Pennsylvania."

WHILE ALL THESE ukulele eminences were emerging on the mainland, another had appeared in Hawaii.

Ernest Kaai was celebrated in the islands as "the Father of the Ukulele." A superb performer on almost every stringed instrument, he was the first to convincingly demonstrate that a melody could be played on the uke entirely with chords. He also wrote the earliest book on ukulele instruction—*Hawaiian Guitar and How to Play It*. That was in 1906, and Kaai followed it with a successor in 1916. *The Ukulele, a Hawaiian Guitar* was a highly sophisticated treatise intended for advanced enthusiasts. Kaai was one of the very few ukists in the world who could master its subtle theories and intricate strumming techniques.

ernest kaai

But Kaai was more than just an inspired player. He was also an assiduous and imaginative promoter. At nineteen, he was already a successful impresario. Up to twelve of the bands he organized and managed were active throughout the islands at the same time. Next he formed the Kaai Ukulele Manufacturing Company, which he sold in 1917. It became the Aloha Ukulele Manufacturing Company. Kaai remained a shareholder, but not for very long. The islands were too confined, too limited for a man with his ambitions. Soon he was on a boat, bound for more spacious worlds of opportunity.

Johnny marvin

JOHNNY MARVIN WAS one of those kids who left home in his teens to join a circus or a carnival or a tent show. In Marvin's case, it was an act called "The Royal Hawaiians." The ukulele was only one of the several instruments on which, at sixteen, he was already adept. On the vaudeville circuit, he sang as well as strummed—his crooning penetrated to the underwear of his listeners. In 1924 he made his first recording as a ukulele and song stylist with "You Know Me, Alabam." After that he became known as "The Ukulele Ace," though he also recorded as "Ukulele Luke" and, on the Harmony label, as "Honey Duke and His Uke."

In 1926, Marvin hit Broadway in a musical called *Honeymoon Lane*. It had a successful run, which triggered a splurge of recording dates. Soon he'd contracted with Harmony to promote a signature Johnny Marvin tenor uke. This venture took him to London, accompanied by ten thousand miniature ukes to be distributed as promotional aids. One, engraved with gold, was presented to the Prince of Wales, and a special model named after His Royal Highness and fashioned from koa wood was soon introduced to the public.

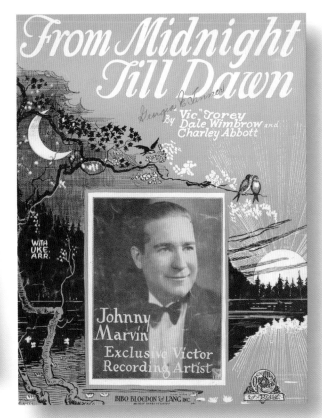

From Midnight Till Dawn

By Vic Torey, Dale Wimbrow and Charley Abbott

WITH UKE. ARR.

Johnny Marvin
Exclusive Victor Recording Artist

BIBO, BLOEDON & LANG INC.

↻ With a winning smile, crooning voice, and skills on the guitar as well as ukulele, Johnny Marvin was a hit with Broadway and vaudeville audiences.

Wendell Hall

1,000,000 · COPY · EDITION · WITH · 24 · NEW · VERSES

It Ain't Gonna Rain No Mo'
by **Wendell Hall**

WENDELL HALL
Exclusive Victor Record Artist

As sung by the National Radio Favorite~
The Composer   On Victor Records

FORSTER MUSIC PUBLISHER INC.

CLIFF EDWARDS, Roy Smeck, Ernest Kaai and Johnny Marvin had all become professional ukists when they were very young. Wendell Hall, the "red-headed music maker" from Kansas, was different. He was well into his twenties before he ever picked up a ukulele. But once he got the hang of it, there was no stopping him.

First he landed a job as an itinerant song plugger, working the music stores, theaters and radio stations throughout the Midwest. Then he graduated to vaudeville, where he played both the ukulele and the xylophone. The uke was much easier for a traveling man to carry from booking to booking, so he soon decided to concentrate mostly on that instrument. He also composed songs and in 1923 wrote and recorded an immense hit— "It Ain't Gonna Rain No Mo'." The title might also have read "It Ain't Gonna Happen No Mo'." No song that Hall later produced ever came close to selling the two million copies rung up by this very early success.

Radio, not songwriting, was Hall's meat and potatoes, his bread and butter. Between 1929 and the late 1930s, he hosted or was frequently featured on three popular variety shows. He was even married in a radio station. The ceremony was conducted on the air in a live broadcast. Though he published an instrumental book, continued to write songs, and designed a line of "Red-Head Ukuleles," he remained essentially a radio and recording figure for the rest of his career.

The Wendell Hall-designed Redhead ukulele.

MOST OF THE great pioneer uke masters were either Hawaiian or American. But one was an incomparable Englishman. His stage name was George Formby, and he was arguably the most successful entertainer ever to perform on the uke.

Formby was nobody's idea of a matinee idol. He was small and scrawny. He had the buckteeth of a chipmunk. He spoke with the broad accent of his native Lancashire, England, which he never attempted to disguise or refine. He was able to carry a tune, but his singing voice was distinguished chiefly by its audacity. His timing was delectable, however, and his smile infectious. His fellow countrymen, millions of them, loved him as they did no other music hall entertainer of his or any other time.

Formby (whose true name was George Roy Booth) came from an illustrious show-business family. In 1921, he took both his father's name (George Sr. was a wildly popular but disenchanted comedian who vehemently opposed any thought of a theatrical career for his son) and his act back on the stage. It was a catastrophe. What had won curtain calls for the father earned catcalls for the son.

But then Formby's future was rescued by the ukulele.

To be more exact, it was a banjo ukulele, which has a more strident voice than a conventional uke and a body more circular than oblong in shape. It belonged to another performer who was willing to sell it for two-and-a-half pounds—about $25 in current American dollars. Other members of the company dared Formby to build it into his act, and he didn't flinch from the challenge. What did he have to lose? So after he'd learned three basic chords, he picked up the uke and walked out onto the stage to see if he could win his bet.

As it turned out, that ukulele was the best investment Formby ever made. The applause was tumultuous and prolonged. From that performance to the last day of his career, Formby and his uke remained indivisible partners. He was as big a hit in the recording studios as he was in the music halls. His discography lists 230 different titles. Most of them reprised his most popular music-hall numbers and were often selections that he'd written himself. Alone or in collaboration, he composed about 300 songs over the course of his forty years in show business.

During World War II, Formby was enlisted by the Allied High Command to entertain service men and women wherever there were airstrips to land the planes that could reach them. After the invasion of Normandy the British General Bernard Montgomery personally invited him to lift the spirits of the frontline troops. It's estimated that he performed for some two million allied troops before the war ended. For these and other contributions, the crown honored him with an Order of the British Empire in 1946. Some people thought he and his ukulele deserved a knighthood.

Over the years, with a "little ukulele in his hands," he became a symbol of the British spirit.

PLAYER'S CIGARETTES

George

george formby

Diverse as they may have been, most of the leading ukists of that era had one thing in common. They were men. But not all of them happened to wear long pants. At least one was a redoubtable woman.

May Singhi Breen, born in 1895, was a New York kid. Her first ukulele was a Christmas gift, which she didn't know how to play and tried to exchange for something she knew how to wear— a bathrobe. When the return was curtly refused she decided to take lessons. It wasn't long before she was skillful enough to start giving them.

With a sisterhood of other young women, Breen formed a ukulele group called "The Syncopators." They landed a radio contract in New York City, and Breen remained a member until she met a successful Tin Pan Alley songwriter named Peter De Rose. He persuaded her to join him in a piano and ukulele act, which included the harmonies of marriage. That launched a radio show of their own called *Sweethearts of the Air,* which ran for sixteen years on NBC.

May Singhi Breen was a gifted performer. She even rendered, in concert, a sixteen-minute "Rhapsody for Ukulele," which had originally been introduced by Paul Whiteman and his orchestra.

But it's not as an instrumentalist that Breen is most widely recognized today. She's best known as an indefatigable advocate of the ukulele. She had the heart and soul of a suffragette and campaigned for the uke's musical virtues as she might have marched for the rights of women to vote. She was an ardent organizer of ukulele clubs and societies. She continued to be a passionate teacher, both in private schools and in her own studio. When the New York Musician's Union remained reluctant to classify the uke as a legitimate instrument, Breen hounded the officials until they finally conceded its musical merits. She wrote books of instruction that pioneered a method of playing the melody rather than just strumming simple chords. She made the first, and the very successful, phonograph recordings of ukulele lessons.

Most significantly, with persistent pressure, Breen convinced doubtful music publishers to include ukulele arrangements with almost every title to come off their presses. Many of those arrangements were her own. That's why the name of May Singhi Breen appears more often as an arranger of American sheet music than anyone ever to jot down the notes. Nobody may have done more to establish the ukulele as something above and beyond a musical orphan.

On the stage, in the recording studios, over the air and before the cameras, the uke was accorded plenty of attention in those days. Obviously, the performers who played it usually commanded the spotlight. But elsewhere, far from Broadway and Hollywood, other very important things were happening. In workshops and in factories all across the country, a revolution was in the making.

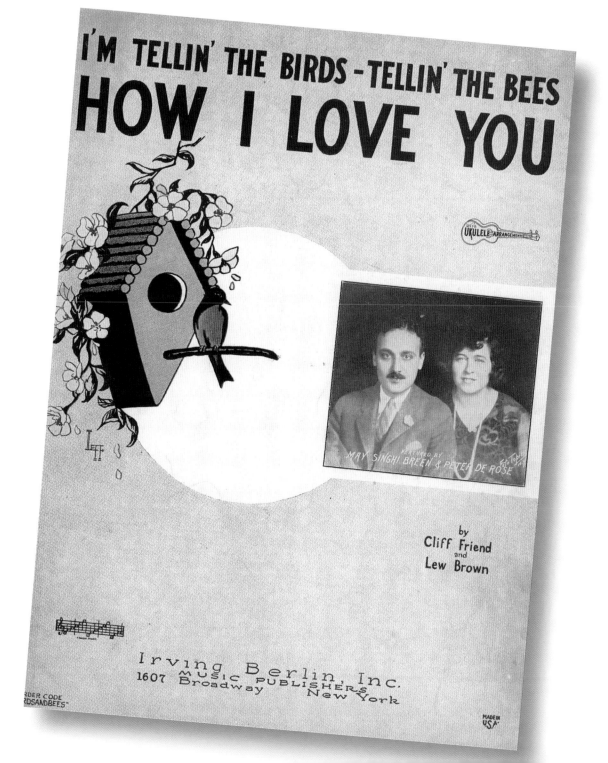

makin' whoopee

The Pioneer Makers and Manufacturers

BACK IN THE ROARING '20s, the word "whoopee" possessed two different meanings. If delivered with a leer and a wink, it suggested certain raptures usually (but not always) confined to the bedroom. Eddie Cantor, a crown prince of vaudeville and musical theater, was able to conjure harems and perfumed bordellos with the rolling of his impudent eyes. One of the hits that made him famous was a highly spiced number called "Makin' Whoopee."

More innocently, "whoopee" was also employed as an exclamation of delight and rejoicing. When a new baby was born or your favorite team won the pennant or your skinflint boss finally gave you a raise, you hollered, "Whoopee!"

The ukulele makers of that era had a lot to celebrate. Between 1916 and the early 1930s they produced and peddled millions of ukes, shouting "Whoopee!" all the way to the bank. During this period, competing brands sprouted as profusely as weeds in midsummer. A recently compiled list, still not entirely complete, numbers over four hundred entries.

Their names were wildly varied and evocative. Some were emotional—Rhapsody, Pleasure, Sunlight. Some claimed advantages of quality—Gold

↶ ↷ As ukes became more popular and the manufacturing price fell, some makers felt the need to adorn the uke with decorations that would reflect the instrument's jaunty personality. Each one is a highly treasured item to ukulele collectors today. Opposite is a La Pacifica, which used a stencil to paint the fanciful Hawaiian scene, while to the right is a Supertone, which used a decal.

Tone, Rich Wood, Triumph, Moore Bettah. Some were endorsed by celebrities—Jimmy Durante, Wendell Hall, Roy Smeck, Johnny Marvin. Some were comic—Howdy Doodie, Uke-A-Doodle, G-String, Kook-a-lele. Many infer a Hawaiian heritage—Islander, Kamaka, Lanai, Maui Maid. At least three were different interpretations of the same seductive word—Waikiki, Wai-ke-ke, Y-keke. Others were simply mysterious—Bean Sprout, for instance, and Digging Stick, and Zen-On. One model, perhaps expressing the maker's response to the exuberant market, was actually called the Whoopie.

Among this multitude of ukes, very few were instruments of any musical distinction. Most were inexpensive novelties, mass produced to satisfy a current fad. Their tone was usually tinny, their workmanship indifferent and their materials ordinary.

To compensate for these deficiencies, the marketers appealed to the eye rather than the ear. They designed ukuleles shaped like a banjo, a pear, a pineapple, a can of tomatoes, a cigar box, even (complete with wings and a propeller) an airplane. Some ukes, like some players, developed a potbelly. One could be played like a violin with a miniature bow.

On top of that, the makers created another form of visual salesmanship. Almost every moderately priced uke was lavishly embellished with imagery. A shopper in those days might have had a choice of a languishing Hawaiian maiden, a comic-strip character like Harold Teen, a simulated

The fanciful Ukalyka, made in England.

tiger hide, a collegiate cheerleader exhorting his team through a megaphone, a couple courting by moonlight, a ghost strumming his triangular uke, a pair of dice turned up to the winning number of seven, a surfer challenging the spray-crested waves, a heaven of stars and moons, of romantic landscapes, all rendered in vibrant color. Entire galleries could and have been crowded with ukulele art.

The more costly and refined the ukulele, the more austere it usually appeared. No vulgar cartoons were exhibited on the bodies of these aristocrats. They were, however, adorned with their own unclamoring enchantments—ebony fingerboards, pearl inlays, even frets of pure silver. These instruments may have been ukes, but they aspired to a formal elegance.

OF ALL the makers operating at that time, the biggest and probably the best was the Martin Guitar Company of Nazareth, Pennsylvania. Martin instruments are venerated for their quality all over the world, but the company's first ukulele was neither an aesthetic nor a commercial success. That was very early, in 1906. In 1916, just after the Pan-Pacific International Exposition ignited the ukulele skyrocket, Martin introduced a second uke. Its guitar sales were sluggish and the troubled company was forced to find other sources of income.

◑ ◐ Ukulele design even went
in the direction of imitation.
This 8-string uke, made by
Lanikai of Hawaii, functions
as either a ukulele or as a
regular 8-string guitar (it
has the standard 19 frets).

This time it hit pay dirt. The new and greatly improved ukulele design, assembled from mahogany rather than from spruce, was an instant hit. Martin was soon selling ukes by the hundreds, then by the thousands. By the mid-1920s, the ukulele rather than the guitar was keeping the brand in business.

At first the Martin ukulele was produced in only one basic edition. Designated as the "Style O," it was a mahogany soprano bluntly described in the company's catalog as "plain, neat, serviceable." It also happened to be quite an exceptional little instrument, and its performance in the marketplace inspired Martin to expand its ukulele line. Before long, the company offered a sequence of four additional models—another more elite soprano, a concert, a tenor and ultimately a baritone. All but the original and unassuming Style-O soprano were available both in mahogany and koa. All but the "O" were richly decorated, and each was progressively more expensive.

⬆ Two ukulele engravings from early Martin catalogs. Photo courtesy of C. F. Martin Archives.

⬅ The C. F. Martin factory in 1925, with Martin ukuleles at the right. Photo courtesy of C. F. Martin Archives.

The bigger the instrument, the higher the price tag.

Martin's promotional literature states that Models 3 and 5 were intended chiefly for professional use. What happened to Model 4? No record of its production or sales figures has ever been discovered. Maybe Model 4 was a thwarted intention. Who knows?

One thing is certain. The Martin 5K was probably the most cherished and celebrated ukulele ever conceived. Over the years, it's become the revered Stradivarius of ukuleles. You could have bought one in the 1920s for $50. Today you'd be lucky to acquire a Martin 5K in reasonable condition for less than $10,000.

↑ **The famous C. F. Martin name appears on the backside of the smaller ukulele headstocks.**

At the peak of its ukulele production, the Martin works turned out twice as many ukuleles as guitars. The factory was obliged to hire extra hands and create extra space. Then a new wing was added, which was later topped by a second story. The company was kept so incessantly busy that it politely declined any special orders, pleading the pressure of previous commitments.

Nevertheless, Martin somehow found the time and the manpower to make ukuleles for other companies. They were as much conspirators as competitors. Martin, for instance, provided some of the merchandise sold by the mail-order giant Montgomery Ward. These were merely competent instruments worth no less and not much more than the very few dollars they cost, and exactly suited to the tastes and the pocketbooks of customers who just wanted to buy themselves some fun.

For quality alone, Martin had no serious rivals during those rip-roaring years. Only two other major manufacturers provided any real competition.

One was the Gibson Company of Kalamazoo, Michigan. Like Martin, Gibson was honored for its meticulously handcrafted guitars. It entered the ukulele market in 1927 with three models of "The Gibson," all fashioned from mahogany. The king of this trio was the Uke-Style 3. It featured a "deep rich mahogany finish," a "rosewood fingerboard bound in white with fancy pearl ornaments," and "seventeen nickel-silver frets," all for the price of $20.

↻ The Stradivarius of ukuleles—one that is considered the finest ever mass-produced—the Martin 5K.

Unfortunately, Gibson delayed the introduction of its ukulele line for too long. The stock market crash of 1929 was only a couple of years away. The Roaring Twenties were soon to become the Depressed Thirties. Gibson ukuleles never had enough time to work up much momentum. The line struggled along for awhile and then quietly expired. It was dutifully mourned by ukulele enthusiasts. "The Gibson" may be gone, but it's certainly not forgotten.

Martin's crown of excellence was also briefly challenged by a second pretender, the Chicago firm of Lyon & Healey. Originally, this was not a manufacturing company. Lyon & Healey were retailers, brokers, agents and packagers. They sensed opportunities and negotiated deals. On the side, they mass-produced the Washburn line of bargain-basement instruments.

As early as 1916, Lyon & Healey began to promote the ukuleles produced in Hawaii by both Manuel Nunes ("the favorite of college men and women everywhere") and Jonah Kumalae. By the 1920s, under the Washburn label, they were marketing their own line of ukuleles, which reached its pinnacle with the extravagantly titled KoaModel 5320 Super DeLuxe. No further adjectives were needed to state that it was a very fine ukulele indeed, and worthy opposition to the superb Martin 5K.

The ukulele aspirations of the Lyon & Healey management, however, were like those of a beer baron who happens to own a champion racehorse. It was more of a hobby than a serious business matter. The company had no intention of pursuing the goal of ukulele supremacy. In 1928, it decided to get out of uke production and concentrate instead on the retail business. All rights, equipment and inventories were

➲ **The Lyon and Healey "Shrine" ukulele.**

↑ Lyon and Healey
"Bell" ukulele.

↑ ↗ The Chicago-based Harmony Guitar Company got into the ukulele business with low-priced ukes, usually decorated with decals and sold through the Sears Roebuck catalog.

sold to another Chicago manufacturer, the J. R. Stewart Company, which plunged almost immediately into bankruptcy.

After an intricate minuet of legalities, the Washburn brand was absorbed by the Regal Instrument Company, also of Chicago. While its name was majestic, its products were anything but. They were cheap. They were gaudy. Their sharp and shallow tone could induce migraine headaches. They were stenciled with cartoons of college boys and sequined flappers and exotic palm trees and a whole universe of come-hither carnival barker hokum.

They were also a whole lot of fun.

Regal produced and sold thousands upon thousands of ukuleles during the '20s and '30s, but nowhere near as many as the Harmony Company, another Chicago instrument manufacturer. Harmony had been the very earliest to mass-produce ukuleles for the avid mainland market. In 1916 the company was gobbled up by Sears Roebuck, which sought to secure a steady supply of ukes for its eager mail-order customers. By 1923, Harmony was churning out some 250,000 instruments a year, many if not most of them ukuleles. Both Roy Smeck and Johnny Marvin were signed to promote their own personal brands. By the late 1920s, Harmony had clearly become the powerhouse of American uke makers.

🡒 The label found inside a vintage Kamaka Pineapple uke.

🡒 Sam Kamaka Sr. took advantage of the times and made ukes for the tourist trade. Photos this spread courtesy Kamaka Hawaii, Inc.

Shoot s/s

MEANTIME, throughout the 1920s, the ukulele manufacturers of Hawaii were sharing the same booming prosperity enjoyed by fellow makers in the United States. The developers, promoters and pitchmen of Hawaii had successfully turned their tranquil islands into an international tourist

attraction. The ocean liners were full of visitors whose pockets were stuffed with expendable dollars. No traveler left Hawaii without having been given an earful of ukulele strumming, and thousands of them carried a just-purchased uke back home either to play or to exhibit as a souvenir. It was on this traffic that the local craftsmen thrived, though their wares were also beginning to infiltrate the retail outfits on the mainland.

Of the Hawaiian makers, three headed the pack.

Manuel Nunes, still falsely claiming to have invented the ukulele, had flourished and brought his boys into the business. It was now advertised as "M. Nunes & Sons." The company produced an ambitious line of ukuleles and other stringed instruments. At the time, its future seemed unclouded at any signs of impending trouble.

Jonah Kumalae didn't perceive any ominous portents, either. His company was doing just fine. The plant occupied half an acre of Honolulu real estate and was busy enough to keep about forty workers on the payroll.

The most efficient and successful maker to emerge in Hawaii, however, was Samuel L. Kamaka. Better than any of his competitors, he combined superior craftsmanship with hard-

☾ A wonderful example of a vintage Kamaka Pineapple uke. Photo courtesy Kamaka Hawaii, Inc.

nosed production know-how. He also had a flair for creative design. His initials were artfully intertwined on the neck of every ukulele the company turned out during its early years. The most famous of them was probably the Kamaka "pineapple uke," introduced by the company in 1916. It was shaped like a pineapple. It looked like a pineapple. But it had a voice that few other ukuleles ever possessed—rich yet robust, elegant yet earthy. Sales continued to soar. The Kamaka family had every reason to feel confident about where their company was headed.

They weren't alone. All the leading ukulele manufacturers at the time were blinded by the same complacency. Not one of them, either in the islands or on the mainland, ever seemed to sense the onrushing catastrophe that was about to engulf almost every one of them.

THE STOCK MARKET CRASH of 1929 caused an immediate panic on Wall Street. The effect of this calamity on the ukulele industry was less immediate, but the results were still crippling and often lethal.

Among the ukulele manufacturers in Hawaii, the Manuel Nunes company struggled on and on, sinking deeper and deeper into the red, until they finally shuttered the business in the middle 1930s. Jonah Kumalae was able to hang on for a few years longer than that. When he passed away in 1940, his company also expired.

What happened to Sam Kamaka's promising business is a happier story. Kamaka didn't die easy. He was a hard, stubborn man, obsessively committed both to the top line of quality and the bottom line of survival. One way or another, he was able to keep his company afloat through the worst years of the Depression and then on through the Second World War.

On the mainland, the Depression's casualty lists were equally grim. Gibson, for instance, first reduced and then totally discontinued its ukulele line. Lyon & Healey unloaded its Washburn line to the J. R. Stewart Company, which itself almost immediately went belly up. Martin's ukulele production numbers, after having climbed to 14,101 in 1926, slumped to 1,987 in 1932. The company remained no better than a listless presence in the ukulele market for the next ten years.

The Regal brand also limped through the middle and late '30s, often producing ukuleles for other companies short of hands and long on cash. It staggered along into the early 1950s, and then finally sold out to the most aggressive of its Chicago competitors, the Harmony Company, which was owned by Sears Roebuck. Harmony was better equipped to weather the rigors of the Great Depression than most of its fellow manufacturers. Nevertheless, it was never a very important listing in the Sears catalogue, and in 1941 Sears ran out of patience with the ukulele. It sold Harmony, together with its subsidiary brands and assets, to a consortium of undaunted employees. The new proprietors managed to keep Harmony alive if not entirely well for another twenty years.

The decline and fall of the ukulele was not caused by the Great Depression alone. Vaudeville had been killed by the merciless competition of movie palaces. Tin Pan Alley had become Swing Street. Sheet music went out of style and its royalties went out the window. Now the jukebox was king. The world danced to a different rhythm these days, sang different songs, moved to a different beat. It was a less innocent world, a more sophisticated world—a world that no longer seemed to have room for a simple little old-fashioned instrument like the ukulele.

But there was a lot of life in the old uke yet.

happy DAYS Are here Again

The Resurgent Ukulele: 1945-1953

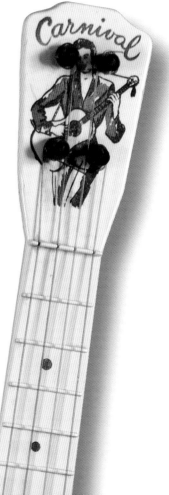

SOMETHING UNEXPECTED happened to the ukulele during World War II. It brought the uke out of dismal obscurity and back into circulation.

At least half a million American servicemen and women saw action in the South Pacific before the Japanese finally surrendered. Coming and going, most of them passed through Hawaii. And you can't visit the islands without getting acquainted with the uke. For many of our warriors, the introduction became a passionate romance. When the troops returned home, thousands came with their decorations, their war stories—and their ukuleles.

Only some of these uniformed enthusiasts bought their ukes in Hawaii. Others waited until after they got settled in the States. Almost immediately ukulele sales soared to numbers they hadn't approached since 1926. Between 1942 and 1944, Martin's ukulele production multiplied by 400 percent. Then, after the first wave of enthusiasm ebbed, the figures dropped back to about the previous levels. There they remained, drifting slightly up or down, until the late 1940s.

Meantime, while the ukeluminaries in America continued to fade

◖◗ The Carnival Plastic Ukulele, with its swell party scenes, cool slang, and low price tag, was perfect for hip youngsters looking for a casual fling with an instrument.

71

into darkness, the irrepressible George Formby went right on wowing his English audiences. The Great Depression didn't slow him down a bit. He was already a musical legend when, after World War II, he also became a movie star. In Hollywood, Cliff Edwards had been featured in bit parts and supporting roles, and Roy Smeck had performed in a few short subjects, but Formby quickly established himself as a leading man. He got top billing and earned top money as well—up to $175,000 per picture. All in all, he and his ukulele lit up the screen in twenty-one comedies. None was an artistic triumph, though all did a very brisk business. Formby was voted Britain's number-one box-office attraction—a more potent draw than Laurence Olivier or Noel Coward. At that time, he and he alone was keeping the uke from sinking even deeper into obscurity.

IT WAS AT THIS POINT, in 1949, that a ukulele Messiah suddenly appeared in the United States.

All by himself, with little or no help from anyone else, this savior was directly responsible for the sale of at least 1,500,000 ukuleles. He introduced the first plastic ukes, and personally demonstrated their depth and color of tone. He played and promoted the ukulele with equal enthusiasm. He summoned all of his wit, all of his wiles, all of his astounding gifts both as salesman and showman to restore the uke to its place in the sun.

You may have heard of this man. His name was Arthur Godfrey.

"The old redhead," as Godfrey liked to describe himself, was a broadcasting prodigy. He had learned to play the ukulele from a Hawaiian shipmate while on sea duty as a radio operator, and while he eventually gave up his Navy career, he never gave up his uke.

In 1929, Godfrey talked his way onto a local talent show run by a Baltimore radio station. The producers liked what they heard. This kid with the ukulele might have a future, they thought. Soon Godfrey was hosting a little radio show of his own, which included occasional on-air uke lessons.

Right from the start, Godfrey turned out to be a one-in-a-million natural broadcaster. His warm, rich, intimate voice never met a microphone it didn't like. Every word he spoke seemed to smile. He became an announcer, but he never announced. Instead, he

◐ This vintage Kamaka ukulele was one of the many ukes purchased in Hawaii by soldiers and brought to the mainland. It is inscribed with "Schofield Barracks," the military post in Hawaii, and with the date "9/1/37." The current owner found the instrument in a secondhand store in New York City and had a Hawaiian scene painted on the back.

arthur
godfrey

confided. He shared his thoughts, feelings, and messages in a way that seemed intended for each listener alone. Nobody taught Godfrey the practice of this art. The gift was instinctive, like an ear for perfect pitch.

His uke was much more to Godfrey than a professional prop or gimmick. Quirky, humorous, unpretentious—it was an ideal partner and an extension of his folksy, down-home personality. Godfrey's musical tastes, like many of his attitudes and opinions, were unapologetically old-fashioned. He favored waltzes and polkas and barbershop harmonies, sweet and simple ballads, uncomplicated chords.

> ➔ **Godfrey tirelessly stumped for the plastic-bodied "Islander" ukulele. It worked; thousands were sold.**

Over the next few years, Godfrey garnered his own coast-to-coast radio shows, which included monologues, interviews with celebrities, guest vocalists backed by an in-house combo—and, of course, Godfrey himself strumming and singing. Then, inevitably, came television—a phenomenon that instantly turned Godfrey into a superstar.

His initial TV venture, *Arthur Godfrey Time,* was launched in 1948. That began an astonishing multiplication of Godfrey TV productions—*Arthur Godfrey and His Friends,* followed by the *The Arthur Godfrey Digest.* By the early 1950s, nine Godfrey shows were watched and heard by some forty thousand fans a week.

It was during this heady period of success that Godfrey decided to turn a part of his radio and TV shows into a ukulele revival meeting. Day after day, week after week, he preached, described and even demonstrated the virtues of the uke. He cut an album of standards, featuring himself and a Vega baritone ukulele. Its title was *Jazz for the People,* and Godfrey sang, strummed and swung. May Singhi Breen, herself a redoubtable ukulele advocate, declared that "the one and only Godfrey" had established the ukulele as "the family instrument of America." Certainly he felt the instrument possessed certain spiritual values. "If he's got a uke in his hands," Godfrey once said, "he's not going to get into much trouble."

He assuredly helped to get the ukulele manufacturers out of trouble. They were hurting. America's ukulele sales were stuck at less than ten thousand a year. It took Godfrey just six months to boost that anemic figure 150,000 percent. And when he began to boost a $5.95 uke called the "Islander," the market exploded.

So did some ukulele purists. The "Islander" was plastic—a material detested and derided by traditionalists. Godfrey didn't care. He savored controversy. He went right on promoting the virtues of the "Islander." Before the campaign was over, he'd helped sell some nine million of these unassuming little instruments to people who might otherwise have never purchased a ukulele at all.

At this time Godfrey was one of the Columbia Broadcasting System's most cherished properties. But in the late 1950s, his popularity crumbled.

On camera, Godfrey was an irresistibly genial and ingratiating personality. Off camera, though, he was increasingly abusive and profane. He had the disposition of a puff adder. Finally, his dark side shadowed the persona he projected on the air when in 1953, during a live broadcast, he ruthlessly fired one of the most popular members of his production family, singer Julius LaRosa. That incident was followed by a barrage of further tirades and dismissals, which poisoned Godfrey's relationships with his bosses, the public and the press. Godfrey furiously defended himself against his critics, but the facts couldn't be masked. His TV ratings began to slump and his health continued to deteriorate. In 1959, revealing that he'd been stricken with lung cancer, he gave up his television and radio shows. He died in 1983, celebrated as much for his bile as for his smile and remembered as much for losing as for winning friends.

tiny tim

AMONG THE MANY millions of people that Godfrey sold on the merits of the ukulele was a strange little kid named Herbert Khaury. His father was Lebanese, his mother Jewish, and he grew up in Manhattan a loner. His best friends were a wind-up gramophone and a stack of records that he played until the grooves were worn away to nearly inaudible scratching. It was the novelty tunes of the twenties and thirties that the young Khaury loved most, and he researched the archives of popular music with an almost Talmudic intensity. By the time he dropped out of high school,

he'd taught himself to play the ukulele. When he became proficient enough, he began to perform as a singer.

His voice, he discovered, was uncommonly flexible. "I was listening to the radio and singing along," he once said, "and it's strange. I can go up high as well as low." He also searched high and low for a professional name. "Herbert Khaury" just didn't sound right for the unique entertainer he hoped to become. He experimented with a series of different identities until finally deciding on Tiny Tim, though nothing about him evoked the lame little boy created by Charles Dickens in *A Christmas Carol.*

To begin with, this Tim certainly wasn't tiny. He was tall, broad-bottomed, swelling plumply at the waist. His hair was long, limp and dyed a lurid red. His dark eyebrows, alluringly arched, gave him the look of a burlesque queen. His smile was broad, constant and slightly goofy. His singing voice traveled back and forth between an unremarkable baritone and a fluttering falsetto. In appearance and in manner, he conveyed an impression of gentle lunacy.

Bizarre as he may have seemed, Tiny Tim was in fact a serious and scholarly man. His knowledge of vintage popular music was comprehensive, and his devotion to its cause was never weakened by adversity. He burned with a great reverence for the songs that he sang. Always courtly, he addressed friends and strangers alike, as "Mister" and "Missus" and "Miss." Bing Crosby once asked him to stop calling him "Mr. Crosby." Tiny Tim smiled. "Okay, Mr. Bing," he said.

In the early 1960s, he negotiated a spot on *Rowan and Martin's Laugh-In,* then one of the top-rated TV variety shows. When he was introduced, he blew flamboyant kisses to the audience, struck an opening chord on his uke, and spiraled away into what later became his signature show piece, "Tiptoe through the Tulips." His act was an immediate sensation. Other opportunities poured in. Tiny Tim followed his debut on *Laugh-In* with several other appearances on the show and then graduated to performances on the even more popular Jackie Gleason, Ed Sullivan and Johnny Carson shows. When he was married on a live broadcast of *The Tonight Show,* forty million people switched on their TV sets to catch the ceremony.

But in the words of a ballad he used to sing, Tiny Tim was "Just One of Those Things." In the limited time that he basked in the spotlight, though, the ukulele shared his intoxicating success.

Tiny Tim was never a very accomplished player. His passion was for the music, not for the instrument. He didn't campaign to promote its sales, never wrote books of instruction, never endorsed models that exploited his few years of fame. He left the hustling of merchandise to Arthur Godfrey and Roy Smeck. They were businessmen. He was simply an entertainer.

Tim kept on entertaining until the day he died—literally. In September of 1996, on stage at a local ukulele festival, Tiny Tim was surprised by a heart attack. He recovered, but the doctors warned him that it might be dangerous to ever perform again. Their admonitions were ignored. Two months later, at the Women's Club of Minneapolis, he suffered a second attack while singing "Tiptoe Through the Tulips." He was rushed to a hospital, but this time the seizure was fatal.

Though Tiny Tim became a celebrity, he was never considered very important. He was a curiosity, a temporary amusement. Most people viewed him as a clown, not as a serious musician. Uke fans argue that his quirkiness seriously damaged the instrument's reputation—though others say he kept the uke alive in the decades after Arthur Godfrey's fame.

If he was ever wounded by the ridicule of his critics, Tiny Tim never displayed any resentment. He endured their barbs with the serenity of a saint about to be martyred. His belief in the music that he played was evangelical, and he offered his antique songs as though they were blessings. He felt that he'd been chosen as the messenger of a truth. In his dedication to that calling, he suffered privation, surmounted humiliation—and, in the end, attained an improbable nobility.

Whole tribes of superb Hawaiian ukists must have been developed during the years that led to the great Godfrey ukulele resurrection. But the islanders aren't very assiduous keepers of their own history. The names of these prodigies may be dimly remembered, but the details of their exploits are confused and uncertain.

There are, however, certain exceptions.

One is Jesse Kalima. He was born in 1920, five years after the uke was triumphantly introduced to the mainland at the Pan-Pacific International Exposition. He was only fifteen when he won the Hawaiian Amateur Ukulele Championship, dazzling the jurors with a rousing treatment of the "Stars and Stripes Forever."

Kalima never took music lessons. Nevertheless, his recordings confirm that he was an amazing technician. He was also a musical pioneer. He originated a distinctive solo style on the ukulele—an approach that combined the playing of chords with the playing of melody. He preferred the mellow, more resonant tone of the tenor uke to the voice of the soprano, and his choice helped to establish the tenor as the favorite of ukulele enthusiasts all over the world. Finally, he was quite possibly the first ukulele virtuoso ever to strum an electronically amplified uke. At the time, this was revolutionary. Today, fifty years later, the benefits of amplification are still the subject of vehement dispute.

During and after World War II, Kalima and a band of his brothers worked USO shows as well as clubs and hotels all over the islands. There were four of them in all. Poi, a staple of the Hawaiian diet, is rich in calories, and none of the group could be described as dainty. Later they often billed themselves as "A Thousand Pounds of Melody."

Kalima was then considered the premier ukulele virtuoso in Hawaii. In 1950, he introduced his own line of ukes—"genuine koa, personally guaranteed." He continued to record and perform until right before he died in 1980. A year later, the Hawaiian House of Representatives passed a resolution honoring his contributions to the culture of the islands.

If Kalima had any serious rival in the years following World War II, it was another Hawaiian virtuoso named Eddie Kamae.

Kamae was born in 1927 and learned to play on an abandoned uke his brother found on the seat of a bus. He grew up to be a small slender man with a gentle smile and an unappeasable hunger to study and master all the potential joys of the ukulele.

As a young amateur, Kamae hung out at the Waikiki Lau Yee Chai Restaurant in downtown Honolulu. Local musicians gathered there to jam and swap trade talk. Often sitting in, Kamae picked their brains as he plucked the strings of his uke. Soon he was ready to turn pro. Together with some of the talent that he met at the restaurant, he formed a group called "The Ukulele Rascals." It wasn't long before he established himself as one of the most gifted players in the islands.

Between performances he continued to explore the ukulele's unknown possibilities. Like Jesse Kalima, he perfected techniques that moved the ukulele out of the background and into the spotlight. Once it had simply been an anonymous member of the rhythm section, but now it was revealed as a lead instrument capable of the most difficult solos. This was a momentous change. Kalima and Kamae together led the charge.

Kamae's assault on convention didn't end there. As he transformed *how* the uke was played, he also transformed *what* was played. The typical Hawaiian repertoire was too primitive and ordinary to satisfy his quests. Seeking new directions, he took advanced courses in musical theory and composition at the University of Hawaii. This equipped him to arrange extremely subtle scores, often difficult to perform. The Ukulele Rascals were up to the challenge. They played music of every kind—folk songs, jazz, Latin sambas and cholas, even classical pieces. It was performed strictly by Hawaiians, but the music itself was international.

Beginning in 1950, Kamae began to double as the featured ukulele soloist with the Orchestra in Residence at the Royal Hawaiian Hotel. It was a sedate and predictable group, leaving well-heeled and deep-pocketed tourists undisturbed by surprises. But as Kamae put his uke through its astonishing paces, he made his audience both sit up and shut up. Few, if any of them, had ever imagined that such sophisticated music could be obtained from so modest an instrument.

Kamae cut an occasional record during this period, but his professional routine remained basically unchanged until 1957. At that point he completely reversed course.

Until then, he had more or less disdained his Hawaiian musical heritage, finding the simple chords and easy progression of the music unchallenging. But in the late 1950s he became an ardent convert. During one of the first jam sessions he had with Gabby Pahinui, with whom he would found the group Sons of Hawaii, he was entranced by the rhythm of Gabby's playing and finally understood why his father had so fervently wanted him to play Hawaiian music. He dissolved the Ukulele Rascals and organized a new band dedicated entirely to the music of the islands. Over the next few years, many of the greatest Hawaiian players signed on as members. Under his leadership, the band became a legend.

For Kamae, however, The Sons of Hawaii fulfilled only some of his deep professional ambitions.

He became an advocate not only of his native music but also of his native culture. In the 1980s he became a filmmaker. With his wife, Myrna, he's since produced a series of acclaimed documentaries on Hawaiian cultural traditions.

Since that time, the Sons of Hawaii have gone their separate ways and have sons and grandsons of their own. Kamae is now in his eighties and has been honored with Lifetime Achievement Awards by the Hawaii State Legislature, the Hawaiian Academy of Recording Artists, the Bishop Museum and the Ukulele Hall of Fame. He's celebrated as a musician, as a historian and as a citizen. He'd be fully entitled to a quiet retirement and the contentment that comes with knowing that his contributions have made a difference. But back there at the start of his career, he promised himself that he'd attempt to find, disclose and demonstrate the almost infinite riches and resources possessed by the ukulele. That was a long time ago, and he's accomplished a very great deal. But he's convinced that there's still a lot of work to do.

ANOTHER IMPORTANT FIGURE in Hawaiian ukulele history was not a native of the islands. He was born in the landlocked and decidedly unromantic town of Omaha, Nebraska, and didn't arrive in Hawaii until he was thirty-two years old. Harry Owens was a musician, but not a performer. He was a composer, an arranger, a manager, a bandleader and a businessman. He'd put together his first orchestra in 1926. Then, in 1934, he was hired by the Royal Hawaiian Hotel to take over as music director.

Owens was instantly infatuated with Hawaii and Hawaiians. He plunged into its culture as though it were a pristine lake and he a man who was dying of thirst. He avidly learned everything he could about

The world-famous Royal Hawaiian Hotel.

traditional and modern Hawaiian music. Many of the songs he discovered and orchestrated had never been transcribed before. It was with memory, not written notes, that the natives often pass their ancient chants from one generation to the next.

In general, the material he collected was divided into two groups. One was the authentic music of the islands, uncontaminated by any foreign influence. The other was called the "hapa hoele" style—a blend of Hawaiian and Western popular songwriting. Owens split his orchestra into two similar sections, each devoted to a different approach. Both sections, though, prominently featured the ukulele. As the Royal Hawaiian Hotel Orchestra became more and more famous, so did the uke. Owens, who presided over the orchestra's rise to eminence, thus became one of the ukulele's best friends.

On top of his bandleading duties and activities, Owens somehow managed to write some three hundred songs. Most of them were Hawaiian in content and spirit. One, "Sweet Leilani," was a smash hit. Crooned by Bing Crosby in a movie called *Waikiki Wedding,* it won the Academy Award for best song in 1937 and topped the Hit Parade charts for twenty-eight weeks. It remains a perennial favorite today, seventy years after Owens wrote it to celebrate the birth of his daughter Leilani.

Throughout the '40s and '50s, Owens led his Royal Hawaiians (including Hilo Hattie) on several ambassadorial tours of the mainland. They were booked into posh venues like the Coconut Grove in Los Angeles and ritzy hotels like the St. Francis in San Francisco. Each of these engagements became to some extent a promotional event for the state of Hawaii—and, by association, a benefit for the ukulele as well. Owens and the orchestra also made regular appearances on a weekly radio show named "Hawaii

Calling," which was beamed to the United States from production studios in the islands. On the air, in the ballroom, on the stage—wherever and whenever the Royal Hawaiians performed, the ukulele always earned a share of the applause.

By the time he died in 1986, Harry Owens had recorded hundreds of sides, one hundred and fifty of them for the Decca label alone. On none of them did he ever play the uke. Other more skillful ukists, though, were invariably there in the orchestra—Owens made certain of that. Even better than some of the greatest players, he understood the essential value of the ukulele. He knew that it had a special way of tempting people to join the party. So it wouldn't have surprised him at all to learn that many of the fans that bought and enjoyed his records also decided to purchase a ukulele of their own. After all, who doesn't want to join in the fun?

Arthur Godfrey, George Formby, Tiny Tim, Jesse Kalima, Eddie Kamae, Harry Owens—all of them helped to rescue and revive the ukulele during the troubled years that followed the Great Depression. But another and very different kind of lifesaver also aided its survival. It wasn't a performer, a bandleader, a personality, or even a man or woman. It was the motion picture industry.

Few of the moguls who ran the Hollywood fantasy factories were crusaders. Most of them were leery of noble causes. They just wanted to make pictures that made money without making trouble or even making their audiences think. It was enough to make them laugh. That's why they made comedies.

One of the best comedies ever filmed was Billy Wilder's *Some Like It Hot,* the story of two scuffling jazz musicians. In desperation and in drag, they join

an all-girls' orchestra on tour. The film would have been a classic even without its most delicious scene—a tiddly Marilyn Monroe rendering "Runnin' Wild" on a uke. The voice on the soundtrack, which is almost as sultry as her silhouette, actually belonged to Ms. Monroe, though the ukulele appears to have been played by somebody else. It doesn't really matter. What really counts is that the uke was assigned a supporting role in a sequence that some enthusiasts feel should have been nominated for an academy award.

Two years later, Paramount released Elvis Presley's most spectacular hit, *Blue Hawaii.* Elvis, festooned by fragrant Hawaiian blossoms and scorched by sunlamps to a tawny bronze, sang the title song, accompanied by the uke. The *Blue Hawaii* soundtrack was the most popular Presley album ever to hit the billboard charts, holding on at number one for twenty weeks.

Jim Beloff's illustrated history of the ukulele has compiled a list of other flicks in which the uke has been a featured player. The first was *Sons of the Desert,* a Laurel and Hardy frolic released in 1933. It was followed by *Waikiki Wedding* (1937), *Coconut Grove* (1938), *Honolulu* (1939), and *A Connecticut Yankee in King Arthur's Court* with Bing Crosby (1949). One way or another, on sheet music covers or movie posters or actually on the screen, Crosby constantly teamed up with the ukulele about as often as he did with Dorothy Lamour and Bob Hope. He met Harry Owens, who relied on the uke to give his Royal Hawaiian Orchestra an authentic Hawaiian voice, sometime before World War II. The two of them remained good friends until Crosby's death on a golf course in 1977. Owens lived on for another nine years before he said his last "aloha" in 1986.

As Beloff also notes, movie posters during those years often picture a star cradling a ukulele that he or she never plays in the film. This was not exactly fraudulent. It was intended to suggest, not to deceive.

The uke was a lighthearted symbol of many fundamental pleasures—of music, of dancing, of laughter, of pretty girls and handsome suitors, of tenderness and wicki-wacki-woo. If the poster featured a ukulele, it didn't make much difference whether or not the stars could actually play it or even if it was never played at all. The uke itself was evidence that the picture was going to offer a lot of good old-fashioned fun.

The uke was to prominently figure in later productions too—in the aforementioned *Blue Hawaii* (1961) with Elvis Presley, in *Butch Cassidy and the Sundance Kid* (1969) with Paul Newman and Robert Redford, in *Pennies from Heaven* (1981) with Steve Martin, in the *Purple Rose of Cairo* (1985) with Woody Allen and Mia Farrow, and perhaps most memorably in *Stanley's Gig* (2000), the sensitive and touching story of a forlorn musician who's hired to play his uke as therapy for the cranky old residents of a retirement home.

All of these films were released later on, after the moviemakers of an earlier era had helped keep the ukulele alive during and beyond the Great Depression. Together with the great players and TV personalities of that time, they formed a kind of rescue squad. It wasn't in any way an organized campaign,

and the uke never quite recovered its former glory. Little by little, though, year after year, it was nursed back to health.

Now it was ready for another great leap into the future.

Jake Shimabukuro
live

say it with music

Contemporary Virtuosos and Personalities

The ukulele has thrived and survived chiefly because of one endearing and enduring attribute. Of all legitimate instruments, it's probably the easiest to play.

The uke possesses only four strings. This makes it far less exacting to locate the desired fingerings than on the six-stringed guitar or the five-stringed banjo. Compared to these more challenging cousins, it's simplicity boiled down.

The uke is a cinch to tune—"my dog has fleas." All ukulele instruction manuals and songbooks are furnished with basic chord diagrams that any musical illiterate can comprehend and follow. With these diagrams as a guide, a novice can learn to play a song in hours and sometimes in minutes. To sound a chord, you simply gently (or not so gently) brush an index finger across the strings. The action produces a warm and friendly sound. Hey, you exclaim, listen to *that!* And listen to *this*—a real chord! All of a sudden, you're making music!

Well, maybe.

Most initiates never advance very far beyond their first rudimentary strumming of the ukulele. They seldom become proficient because they don't bother to practice. Why should they? If they fumble away a note, if they mistake a chord, if they lurch off the beat—hey, who cares?

◗ The cover of Jake Shimabukuro's *Live* album shows the ukulele virtuoso in his element. Image courtesy Jake Shimabukuro.

Everybody's having a good time. That's all that really counts, isn't it?

There's little doubt that this indulgent attitude has shadowed the ukulele's reputation. Musical elitists rarely forgive any lapse of discipline or failure of purpose. The critics therefore presume both the instrument and its players to be amusing but trivial. Ironically, the same characteristics that make the uke so universally appealing are the traits that cause it to be so severely snubbed.

While the uke is surpassingly easy to play freely, it's surprisingly difficult to play very well. Its simplicity can be a handicap to performers of subtle and complex works. Only a few masters have elevated the ukulele to concert status. Most people sense that the uke has its own cheerful and ingratiating character. The leading virtuosos, though, are out to prove that it also possesses a passionate soul.

SINCE THE 1920S, several great Hawaiian ukists have dedicated themselves to a kind of crusade. They believe that the ukulele can voice colors and textures and depths of feeling that almost nobody else ever thought possible. These were more than exceptionally accomplished players. They were musical visionaries.

Among the earliest of these remarkables was and is Bill Tapia. Just one of the astonishing facts about Tapia is that he, his mother, his father and an aunt all share the same birthday. Even more amazing, though, is his longevity. He's still performing in clubs and in concerts at the nearly impossible age of 102.

BILL TAPIA

"Tappy," as some people call him, was born in Honolulu on January 1, 1908. He was taught his first chords at the age of seven, and by thirteen he was already playing with legends like Ernest Kaai. He worked in vaudeville, theaters, saloons, and on cruise ships—wherever he could land an engagement. Later on, the Royal Hawaiian Hotel hired him as a combined chauffeur and troubadour. He both drove and serenaded the guests (though not at the same time). Not even his gifted hands were able to simultaneously manage the wheel and massage the uke.

Tapia made his share of recordings, but he hasn't been as aggressively courted by the studios as some of his fellow prodigies. He eventually moved to Southern California, which—with frequent visits to the Islands—has been his home ever since. Between gigs, he gave ukulele lessons to Shirley Temple, Jimmy Durante, and even Clark Gable. All these years, he's continued to refine and extend his skills. He keeps very busy.

In January of 2008, Tapia was honored at a sold-out celebration of his one hundredth birthday and eighty years as an apostle of the ukulele. It wasn't billed as a farewell performance, and has since been followed by similar events. Tapia isn't ready to tap out quite so soon. He still has some strumming to share.

MEANTIME, back in the early 1940s, another phenomenon surfaced in Hawaii.

At seven, tutored by his mother, Herb Ohta learned his first chords on the uke. Before long, he was a more-than-competent strummer. By the time he was ten, he was winning every amateur contest in sight. He was so skilled, in fact, that the producers of one radio show refused to let him perform against competition he was certain to defeat.

With his uke on the beach one day, he happened to encounter the iconic Eddie Kamae. "Play me something," Kamae suggested. The kid responded with a dazzling rendition of the "Stars and Stripes Forever." Kamae was confounded. He instantly adopted the juvenile as a protégé—almost as an heir. He introduced the Japanese-American kid to a universe of opportunities and challenges—classical compositions, popular songs, folk music, mambos, sambas and bossa novas, even flashy Spanish flamencos.

Herbert Ohta didn't remain an intern for very long. He quickly mastered every lesson he was given. "There's nothing more I can teach him," Kamae pretty quickly confessed.

This didn't mean that Ohta stopped learning. He studied music theory at the University of Hawaii, where he eventually graduated with a degree in sociology. He continued to experiment, explore and discover. Like the early Portuguese mariners, he carried his stringed instrument to places it had never before visited.

But the years that followed World War II were very tough for the music and entertainment business. The world was just beginning to recover from twenty years of depression, death and destruction. To support himself, Ohta enlisted in the United States Marine Corps at the age of twenty-one. He was later stationed in Japan, serving as a military interpreter. There he met a leading Japanese musicologist who arranged his first recording session and helped promote his

herb ohta

STEREO
74704
CCA
OHTA SAN

UKULELE ISLE

TOO MUCH
ADIOS KE ALOHA
TWILIGHT IN TOKYO
LITTLE BROWN GAL
EBB TIDE
DAHIL SA IYO
I'LL REMEMBER YOU
UKULELE ISLE
PEARLY SHELLS
HAWAIIAN WAR CHANT
HERE IS HAPPINESS
LEGEND OF THE RAIN

RECORDED IN HAWAII

initial public concert. It was a start, but only a start. In 1955, he got another break—a guest shot on the Ed Sullivan TV show, when he electrified the audience with a treatment of the Latin classic "Malaguena." After that, nothing very notable happened until, after a ten-year stretch, he said "aloha" to the Marine Corps and returned to Hawaii.

In his younger years, Ohta had the smoldering soulful eyes and the sculptured pompadour of a Polynesian Elvis Presley. The first album he recorded in Hawaii, for the historic Hula label, became a Presley-like hit. One of the cuts, written by Ohta himself, was called "Sushi." The Hawaiian public ate it up. It soared to the top of the charts in the Islands and also did well when it was released as a single in the States.

It was at this time that a top executive of Hula Records persuaded Ohta he should no longer bear the burden of being called "Herbert." So, like the

Hollywood moguls who invented glamorous names (and sometimes whole life histories) for their movie stars, he proposed to market this ukulele artist simply as Ohta-San—a far more alluring and distinctive identification. To the Japanese, "san" is a term that signifies deep and abiding respect. To that very important segment of his audience, it immediately identified him as an eminence. He's been known as Ohta-San ever since.

Despite the success of his debut album, the next few years were a disheartening struggle for Ohta-San. He continued to record with Hula Records, but his royalty checks barely covered the cost of new ukulele strings. Just to get by, he was obliged to work in dark and dubious clubs for next-to-nothing wages. For a time he seriously considered finding another line of work—maybe something connected with his degree in sociology. But once again, destiny intervened. In the club where he was then playing, an insistent young man convinced him to persist. "You're too good to be playing in dives like this," the stranger exhorted. "Take me on as your agent. I can get you the kind of bookings and the money you deserve."

Agents have been making and breaking promises of this sort almost forever, but for once the agent actually delivered on his schemes. Soon Ohta was a fixture at a posh Honolulu hotel where he was guaranteed $2,000 per week, plus a split of the take after expenses. That often boosted his income to between $4,000 and $5,000 a week. Ohta-San was on his way to bigger and better things, and so was his youthful impresario. Seeking even richer possibilities, he moved to California. There he shrewdly and swiftly made enough money in real estate to retire at age thirty-three.

The newly christened Ohta-San, then in his middle twenties, had no such longings for early retirement. He plunged into a prodigious recording binge that produced over seventy albums, singles, and CDs

and isn't over yet. In the early 1970s, he cut a piece written expressly for him by the eminent French composer and conductor André Popp. It was called "A Song for Anna," and it became a bonanza for Ohta-San. At last count, it had sold over six million copies—far more than any ukulele disc ever released.

Over the years, Ohta-San has toured and performed the music of many different countries. The diversity of his repertoire is astounding. One of his most recent CDs offers magisterial interpretations of pieces by Johann Sebastian Bach—works usually reserved for the harpsichord or the piano. He has a special interest in the music of Japan, the land of his ancestors. Just as he's adopted their music, they've adopted him. He's immensely popular in Japan, where he frequently performs and has also profusely recorded.

Ohta-San is more than a great player of the ukulele. He's also a prolific and accomplished songwriter and composer. Many of his compositions are intricate studies, almost but not quite classical in their effect, and are not intended for casual listening. They require the strict and silent attention of work performed in the salon, the auditorium, or the concert hall.

Ohta-San has been showered with honors, both as a player and as an arranger. In 2006, the Hawaii Academy of Recording Arts gave him a Lifetime Achievement Award as a ukulele virtuoso. That same year, the Ukulele Guild of Hawaii officially pronounced him a national treasure. And to top it all off, he was installed in the Ukulele Hall of Fame in the United States.

Ohta-San is no longer the slender sexpot he was in his twenties. His torso has gradually thickened and his dark eyes observe the world through owlish spectacles. He's pleased with the successes he's attained. But of them all, maybe the most satisfying has nothing to do with hit recordings, with coveted awards, or with the acclaim of infatuated audiences. Ohta-San has produced an Ohta-Son. Herb Ohta Jr. is a ukulele prodigy in his own right. He may or may not ever be as accomplished as his old man, but it really doesn't seem to matter. He prefers to work as a composer, arranger and producer, remaining behind the spotlight.

One day, perhaps, he'll be known as Ohta-San Jr. Ohta-San Sr. would like that.

BACK IN THE 1920s, the immortal Jelly Roll Morton wrote and recorded a tune called "Dr. Jazz." The lyrics celebrated both a new kind of music and also a new system of communication, the telephone.

"Hello Central, give me Dr. Jazz!
He's got what I need, I'll say he has!"

Morton, never a man to understate his own importance, considered himself to be the unchallenged Dr. Jazz of his time. His lips were rarely soiled by praise for colleagues and competitors. But if he were still around to pronounce his opinion, even he might have to concede that Lyle Ritz is indeed the Dr. Jazz of the ukulele.

Ritz doesn't possess the eagle eye or the chiseled features of a pathfinder. He's edging into his eighties now and is watching his step. He's neither tall nor short, neither plump nor slim, neither pale nor dark. An ordinary man, some people might suppose. But as soon as he picks up the ukulele, he becomes a giant.

At the time Ritz first started to play the ukulele, the instrument was still presumed to be a harmless absurdity. Ritz was an authentic pioneer. What he intended to settle was not a territory but an issue. Was it possible to play jazz, genuine jazz, on the uke? Other ukulele virtuosos have flirted with that elusive possibility, but Ritz pursued it with the ardor of a true believer. In the end he answered it, once and for all. The argument is over.

Ritz was born in 1930. That was in Cleveland, Ohio, a town and state generally congenial to the ukulele. As a kid he played the violin, not the uke. When he was drafted into the Army during the Korean War, he switched to the tuba and then to the acoustic bass. Before long, he was playing in service groups with pros like Lenny Niehaus, another draftee who'd worked as Stan Kenton's lead alto saxophone before Uncle Sam put him in a uniform.

Later, restored to his civvies, Ritz and his bass drifted in and out of various orchestras throughout the 1950s. He continued to get better and better, but opportunities continued to get worse and worse. The Big Band era was already down and on its way out. To keep himself in groceries, Ritz took a part-time job at the Southern California Music Company in Los Angeles. It was there that he first started to fool around with the uke.

What began as a casual interest soon became a serious study. Ritz bought himself the type of ukulele he still plays today, a Gibson tenor, and soon became an exceptionally proficient chordist. Practicing in the store one day, he was overheard by a rep for a then obscure label, Verve Records, who offered him

LYLE RITZ

a recording gig. Ritz worked up some material, toted his Gibson into the studio, and smoothly laid down two unaccompanied albums.

The first, *How About Uke?*, was released in 1958. The second, *50th State Jazz*, came out a year later. Neither did very much business. But among dedicated and informed ukists, and especially in Hawaii, these issues created a sensation. Nothing like them had ever been heard before. The effect was revolutionary. The jazz ukulele had finally arrived.

By this time, however, Ritz had become equally skilled on the bass. He became one of the trade's legendary "Wrecking Crew"—an elite corps of freelance musicians who shuttled constantly from studio to studio, often working several sessions a day. When you wanted the best bass player you could get in Los Angeles, Lyle Ritz was at the top of the list.

Over the next twenty years, he was hired for more than five thousand different recording dates. Jazz, rock, pop, movie scores, radio and television commercials—Ritz played them all. He backed many of the hits recorded by Frank Sinatra, Linda Ronstadt, Herb Alpert, the Righteous Brothers, Ray Charles, Sonny and Cher, the Beach Boys, Tina Turner and Johnny Mathis. He was kept so busy on the bass that he had to mothball his ukulele. Only once during this period did it come out of the closet for a professional session. That was when he supplied the chords behind Steve Martin's pantomimed strumming in a movie called *The Jerk*.

The life of a successful studio musician is lucrative but strenuous. At sixty, Ritz was feeling the strain. Besides, he was itching to renew his languished love affair with the ukulele. So he shut up shop in Los Angeles, took a deep breath, and then moved to the more relaxed climate of Hawaii.

Located there on the island of Oahu, he inevitably ran into Ohta-San. The two virtuosos greatly admired each other but had never met. Soon they became good friends. They often played together in private for pure pleasure and occasionally in public for pride and profit. Then and later they also teamed up in the recording studios. Sometimes they performed as a ukulele duet, sometimes with Ritz supporting Ohta-San's uke on the bass.

Like the solos that Ritz recorded for Verve in the late 1950s, these discs are treasured by the ukulele cognoscenti. They transcend the simple knack of improvisation. They accept a theme and then proceed to shape it, to structure it, and finally to transform it—to create, in fact, new and different themes of their own. What they offer is that mysterious alchemy of discipline and discovery called jazz.

Bass players are often reticent. It's their nature to remain in the background. Ritz found fortune in that inconspicuous role, but not fame. For twenty years his only recorded ukulele works were those two unheralded albums released in the 1950s by Verve. Yet, little by little, year after year, *How About Uke?* and *50th State Jazz* continue to exert an insistent and ever-widening influence. Ritz himself had no idea that he was being elevated almost to some kind of musical sainthood. He first became aware of his celebrity when he moved to Hawaii and heard himself described as "a living legend." This extravagance made him uncomfortable. "I'm living, all right," he says. "Let's just leave it at that."

These days, Ritz goes on living (and leaving it at that) in Portland, Oregon. Portland is noted for the beauty of its roses, for the incandescent support of its NBA basketball team, and also as a seething hotbed of ukulele enthusiasts. Annual ukulele seminars and festivals are staged in Portland. Ritz is one of the main attractions, as he is at other ukefests here and there across the country and in Hawaii. He also teaches. He's collaborated with his friend Jim Beloff on a book of ukulele instruction. And, at cautiously spaced intervals, he continues to record.

For these sessions he almost never returns to the lavishly equipped studios in which he made his living for two decades. He'd labored for years to perfect a homemade recording system capable of satisfying his very exacting standards. Nothing he tried measured up. Then, in 2005, he acquired a computer program called "Garage Band." Buried in its entrails were the answers he'd been seeking, but it took months of arduous research before he was able to fathom and finesse the technology. Finally, though, he was ready to record his first CD on the process he'd been building.

No Frills is the name of the album. Released in 2006 by the Flea Market Music label, it was created entirely by Ritz and his computer in a spare room of his house in Portland. Ritz was the only performer. He played the uke and a synthesis of two different basses, one a stand-up acoustic and the other electronic. Among ukaholics, and especially to the addicts of ukulele jazz, this was a notable event. They'd been waiting to hear something new from Ritz for a long time, and at last that something new had arrived.

Today, however, they continue to wait for his next achievements. Ritz rations his recordings with an almost reluctant restraint. He dispenses each offering like sips of rare cognac from a small and secret supply. This seems to intensify the response. Alcohol can rush to the head when taken on an empty stomach. The less available the product, the more valued its creator.

In 2007, Ritz was enshrined in the Ukulele Hall of Fame, where he joined his friend Ohta-San and other fellow titans. Modestly accepting the honor at the Portland Ukulele Festival, he didn't seem much surprised. By now, it seems, he's getting used to the accolades.

NO UKIST in the business has experienced a career more active, more diverse or more improbable than Ian Whitcomb. He's a handsome man—tall, slender and sinewy, with glinting blue eyes and abundant sandy hair flecked with gray. Whitcomb is now in his late sixties, but he has the look of a retired tennis pro who's still fit enough to give an amateur club champion thirty years his junior three sets of very stiff competition. This casual elegance is deceptive. Neither his manner nor appearance suggest that Whitcomb is a man who probably knows more naughty vaudeville music hall songs than any performer alive, or that in the 1960s, before he reformed and switched from the guitar to ukulele, Whitcomb was a genuine rock star.

Whitcomb was born in England. His family was a menagerie of irregulars. One of his grandfathers founded a British automobile insurance company, made millions, and set himself up as a grandee with a mansion in London and a holiday castle in Scotland, with liveried chauffeurs and servants, and then proceeded to squander this splendor on dubious speculations. He died bankrupt.

But Whitcomb's other grandfather shrewdly preserved the money he made in his father's oil business. He was a connoisseur of Scotch whiskey and also of music hall ditties, many of them shaded with sexual innuendo. Whitcomb was too young to be instructed in the joys of alcohol, but his grandfather taught him many pungent numbers that he still plays and sings today. This education in popular music was further advanced by a great aunt's marriage to a raffish songwriter, who taught Whitcomb some of the tricks of his trade. At first the family judged the match unsuitable, but their objections to the bridegroom were eventually dispelled by the royalties that

ian whitcomb

comb band." The description is vague, but the clear inference is that it wasn't very good. For Whitcomb, band organization became a lifelong habit. After he graduated, he formed another group called the Ragtime Suwanee Six, which toodled pop songs and Dixieland standards in raucous pubs and at decorous garden parties. Then he proceeded to Trinity College in Ireland. "It was easy to get into," Whitcomb confides. There he promptly assembled a third outfit, Warren Whitcomb's Bluesmen, while occasionally attending lectures on history and political science on the side. "Warren," Whitcomb felt, sounded less stodgy than "Ian."

This was in the early 1960s. The Beatles had rocked-and-rolled both England and the United States into a delirium. Whitcomb looked, listened, learned and veered away in new directions. He toured the United States—the first of his many Atlantic crossings between the land of his birth and the country he later adopted. By now he was playing not only the piano but also the accordion, the amplified guitar—and, once in awhile, almost as a joke, strumming the uke.

Back in Ireland, he put together yet another band, Bluesville Manufacturing. In 1963, he led this group into a squalid basement that defiantly called itself a recording studio, where they produced an album that contained a novelty composed by Whitcomb himself. He wasn't especially proud of it. "I thought it was junk," he admits.

Maybe it was, but junk sometimes sells like pure gold. Exported from Ireland to Southern California,

flowed from compositions like "Lady of Spain" (a perennial accordion favorite) and "Let's All Sing Like the Birdies Sing."

Though Whitcomb's father had his financial ups and downs, he made sure that the young Ian was given proper piano lessons. Whitcomb was an indifferent student. Even now he has trouble reading those little black notes. But by the time he was in his teens and sent off to an expensive private school, he learned enough to negotiate almost any popular song he happened to favor.

When he enrolled, about the first thing Whitcomb did was to organize what he calls a "lavatory and

Whitcomb's piece of "junk" was released by Tower Records as "You Turn Me On." It instantly turned on the American market, climbing to #8 on Billboard's national charts. When he flew from England to the United States, Whitcomb was mobbed at the airport. All of a sudden, thanks to his piece of "junk" and the inscrutable workings of fate, he became what he wanted most to be—a rock star.

During those heady days, Whitcomb was interviewed on many of the top-rated TV programs. He recorded another album, and then still another. He toured with the Rolling Stones and the Beach Boys. And toward the end of this period, he produced an album for the incomparable Mae West, a six-month experience he remembers as one of his most exhilarating. He also performed at the Hollywood Bowl as part of an all-star lineup that included Sonny and Cher. Unfortunately, the sound system failed at the moment Whitcomb appeared on stage. His material was good, but nobody was able to hear a word he said or a note he played.

It was an ominous portent.

For a while his career thrived. Then it dived. Throughout the '60s, as rock-and-roll ceased rocking-and-rolling, he drifted from gig to inglorious gig. Finally, in the early '70s, he had to face the facts. If he was going to make his living as a musician, he'd have to find a different way to do it.

And there it was, nestled in its case, ready for the rescue.

So now it was back to the future. Whitcomb had always been a lover of the British music halls, of American vaudeville, and of the music inspired by the Roaring Twenties. This was his chance to become an altered Ian Whitcomb, a reformed Ian Whitcomb, a Whitcomb who at last had returned and been reconciled with his old friend, the uke.

What he's managed to achieve between then and now is nothing short of amazing.

He's recorded forty-six albums, most of them featuring the ukulele. The selections are gathered from many different sources and eras. Whitcomb favors the tunes of Tin Pan Alley, but doesn't discriminate against Latin rhythms or country western material. If it sounds good, if it feels good, if it's right for the uke—hey, bring it on.

In recent years, some of Whitcomb's most satisfying work as a songwriter has been commissioned by the movies. He wrote and played (off-screen) most of the songs used in *Stanley's Gig*, the story of a woebegone ukulele pro

In the summer of 1966, Whitcomb appeared on the TV show *Where The Action Is*, playing the uke on the beach in Malibu. Whitcomb kept the uke in the pop culture eye during the time between Arthur Godfrey and Tiny Tim. Images courtesy Ian Whitcomb.

who lands a job in a retirement home. About an hour's worth of his material was built into *The Cat's Meow,* directed by Peter Bogdanovich. Another film, *The Last Call,* stars Sissy Spacek and Jeremy Irons and contains thirteen Whitcomb originals. Most of these compositions are featured in his various songbooks.

In Los Angeles as in England, Whitcomb has energetically organized several bands. Two of them remain active. One is a ritzy ten-piece dance orchestra that performs in evening clothes and executes the intricate arrangements of the jazz age with impeccable precision. The other group, The Bungalow Boys, consists of five pieces, including Whitcomb himself. They work pretty regularly at private parties and public events, and have also become a popular fixture at a local restaurant. The boys cheerfully accept requests. The patrons sing along. The cash registers work overtime. It's as close to a permanent gig as the uncertain music business can provide these days.

Over the years, Whitcomb has hosted three radio shows of his own. One was in England, the other two in Los Angeles. He's still on the air today, once a week, chatting with his pals, spinning his vintage records, pronouncing his opinions and dispensing his charm.

WHITCOMB has become a great hero of the ukulele, but he's no virtuoso. He strums chords, left-handed, seldom if ever attempting any single note acrobatics. Asked to identify his most-important musical asset, he simply holds up his index finger. Whitcomb, is, in fact, essentially neither a player nor a performer. He's something more than that. He's a natural, instinctive, obsessive entertainer. Even as a kid, his hunger to entertain was apparent. This urgent need has never abated. After one of his dates, you don't hear people say, "Wasn't his playing beautiful?" What they say instead is, "Wasn't that a whole lot of fun?"

Whitcomb has mellowed over the years. He savors the quiet comforts of a regular life with his wife, Regina, who's a very good cook and an excellent singer. He writes his books. He runs his radio show. He records his albums. He prunes his fruit trees and pampers his pets. Meantime, like a volcano, he continues to seethe. His energy, his drive, can't be contained. When and where will it overflow next?

HIS TONGUE-NUMBING LAST NAME is Shimabukuro, but almost everybody in the ukulele universe simply calls him "Jake." And almost everybody agrees that he's one of the greatest—possibly *the* greatest—ukulele virtuoso ever to visit the planet.

More than any of his predecessors or contemporaries, this young Japanese-American has boosted the uke to a new and rarefied level. He treats it like a concert instrument and is himself accepted as a concert artist. Like a Segovia on a guitar or a Rubenstein on the piano, he stars as a soloist. On tour, he's sometimes backed by a small ensemble, but he is more often accompanied by intricate arrangements performed and

Jake Shimabukuro

Photo by Hisashi Uchida,
courtesy Jake Shimabukuro.

recorded in advance. In these performances, attended by hundreds if not thousands of fans, he alone occupies the stage, he and his ukulele.

Out in the spotlight, Jake mixes the antics of a rock star with the etiquette of a classical musician. He usually appears in a t-shirt and jeans. They make him look sleekly athletic, though not scruffy. Jake is small, but obviously very strong and agile. He's wired for sound so that he can move around at will. In the middle of an exuberant jazz or rock selection, he's been known to leap from the stage and plunge into the audience. These incidents are never rehearsed. "They just happen," Jake says. "I like to have fun up there." But fun for Jake can also be more decorous. While playing a piece by Paganini, for instance, his manner can be a model of exquisite restraint. How he behaves depends on his material, his mood, and the attitude of his listeners.

The Shimabukuro family emigrated from Okinawa to Hawaii five generations ago. Music has always been an important part of their lives. Like several of his fellow virtuosos, Jake's career commenced on a uke given to him by his mother. That was when he was only four years old. "When I played my first chord," he remembers, "I was hooked." Obsessed might be a better description. In school, his only close friend was always the uke. He practiced, practiced, practiced. And, with almost scientific zeal, he probed the possibilities of the ukulele. "That's when I started experimenting with amplifiers, with wah wah pedals, distortion boxes," he says. "I'd try to come up with new ways of playing the instrument so that I could execute different styles of music, like trying to play in a flamenco style or blues."

As he explored the frontiers of the ukulele, Jake was obliquely influenced by the masters of other arts. "It wasn't just musicians who inspired me," he says. "It was anyone who had a unique approach to an art

form. Another one of my heroes was Bruce Lee. I read many books about his philosophy, and I applied a lot of those theories and ideas to the ukulele."

Ordinary strummers may find it difficult to understand exactly how a study of martial arts can advance a player's skills, but nobody can argue with the results of Jake's abstruse methods. He's a brilliant technician. Over the years, he's originated and perfected his own strumming and fingering systems. He usually plays with his thumb and three fingers—sometimes even four. At first he favored a pick, but not any longer. "I use both the fleshy part of my fingers and the narrow part to get different tones," he explains. He's also learned to employ the body of his uke as a drum, and on certain pieces becomes a percussionist and a ukist at the same time. He was, in fact, a drummer in his high school marching band. "I love the rhythms," he recalls. "I've always tried to keep my mind open to different sounds."

Soon after he graduated from high school, Jake wangled a weekly gig at a Honolulu restaurant. Then he signed on as a member of a trio called Pure Heart, which for a while was a pure pleasure for him. It established Jake as a professional performer, and its first two albums earned a whole bouquet of Hawaiian broadcasting and entertainment awards. But despite its early success, the combo eventually gave up on itself. So Jake helped organize another group called Colon. It too was a hit. "Hoku," the Hawaiian counterpart of the Grammy Awards, cited it as the Entertainer of the Year in 2001.

Jake was now twenty-five. It was at this point that he decided to go out on his own as a soloist. That move triggered the ascent of the Shimabukuro rocket.

Since then, Jake has toured the United States, Canada, Europe, Australia, the South Pacific and Asia. In Japan, where his recording company and most important sponsors are based, he's become an

authentic superstar. Jake is so popular with the Japanese that he serves as an official goodwill ambassador for the state of Hawaii and helps to promote its tourist trade wherever he goes. Sometimes he travels with his own small groups, sometimes as part of an elaborate troupe featuring other headliners like Jimmy Buffet and Tommy Emanuel. He's performed for intimate audiences in elite jazz clubs and for over thirty thousand people packed into football stadiums. His signature CD, *Gently Weeps,* has sold more than one hundred thousand copies worldwide. He's also released an instructional DVD, *Play Loud Ukulele,* which sets forth some of his basic beliefs and demonstrates his techniques. Somehow or another, he finds the time and energy to do some long-distance running, and in 2006 even entered and completed the annual Hawaiian marathon. The event's theme song was played over the loud speakers as he crossed the finish line. It was a track selected from his own definitive album *Gently Weeps.*

Jake's achievements have been enthusiastically acclaimed, but the hymns of praise haven't been universal. Some mutterings of dissent have been heard. They come almost entirely from the unyielding traditionalists who believe it a heresy to amplify the ukulele. Any uke that's wired is disdained, and any player who plugs it into an outlet is discounted. Electronics, these critics insist, distort and cheapen the warmth of the ukulele's natural voice. Until he renounces his amplified Kamaka in favor of an acoustic uke, Jake will never convince the purists that he should be rated as one of the world's premiere virtuosos. While they concede that he's a gifted performer, they complain that he fails to respect the integrity of the instrument itself.

This dispute between the traditionalists and the modernists has agitated the ukulele world since amplification first came along. The issue may never be entirely resolved. Certainly the amplified uke isn't about to go away.

Jake is not a contentious man and prefers to side-step the controversy. He is, however, acutely sensitive to the tonal qualities of his ukuleles, which are custom made for him by the Kamaka Company in Honolulu. In subtle but significant ways, many are different from each other. Jake works with one Kamaka tenor in the recording studio, with another in concert performances. Blindfolded, he can instantly identify any of them by the shadings of its tone.

Singers often protest that nothing is more difficult to perform than the "Star-Spangled Banner." For a ukulele player, the challenge is even more daunting. Most people believe it ridiculous to even attempt a treatment of the national anthem on the uke. Nevertheless, Jake decided to prepare his own version of the "Star-Spangled Banner." If you ever hear it, you won't wince with embarrassment or slump silently in your seat. You'll do what the playing of the national anthem is supposed to make you do. You'll probably stand up and cheer.

"Kamakawiwo'ole" is a name almost impossible for any mainlander to pronounce. Even native Hawaiians find its many syllables laborious. They prefer to call Israel Kamakawiwo'ole by a briefer nickname. They refer to him as "Iz."

Iz is unique among the great young uke masters of today. The others are all still living. Tragically, he died in 1997 at the premature age of thirty-eight.

He was an immense man—immense in his girth, immense in his talent. His large fingers could summon from the ukulele an exquisite delicacy of tone unattainable to most other players. And from his vast bulk issued a high sweet voice that seemed almost angelic in its purity. But Iz was carrying too much weight for his heart and arteries to handle. In the end, obesity helped to kill him.

At the time of his death, Iz was a celebrated figure in Hawaii. Elsewhere, though, he was known chiefly for a single album—*Facing Future*. And on that album he's remembered for his haunting and idiosyncratic medley of "Over the Rainbow" and "What a Wonderful World." Here he gently retrieves the song from Judy Garland's tenacious grasp and transforms it into a creation of his own. If he'd never produced anything else, this record would have ensured him some pedestal in the ukulele Valhalla.

FACING   FUTURE

IZ
ISRAEL
KAMAKAWIWO'OLE

He's gone now, gone to join the bluebirds that fly over the rainbow. If you want to send him a message, don't address it to Israel Kamakawiwo'ole. Just "Iz" will get it there.

So far, this discussion has been confined to the greats who performed chiefly as soloists. But there are also superb ukulele *groups* who strut and strum their stuff out there.

The Ukulele Orchestra of Great Britain is perhaps the most illustrious example of the ensemble art. It's composed of seven members, men and women. They usually appear impeccably attired in evening clothes, as though for a coronation or a royal wedding. Their renditions of highly intricate and exacting arrangements are equally impeccable. This is how the ukulele sounds when it's puttin' on the Ritz.

Another notable group, the Langley Ukulele Ensemble, is headquartered in Canada. It's part of the school program designed by J. Chalmers Doane, then the Director of Musical Education in Halifax, Nova Scotia. That was in the 1970s. At one point, about fifty thousand aspiring young ukists were enrolled in Doane's ukulele classes, not only throughout Canada, but also in the United States.

The Langley Ensemble Group is a child of that program. It consists mostly of gifted kids, seasoned by a sprinkling of adults. Their ages range from thirteen to twenty-five. Now and then, the ensemble is joined by the Canadian virtuoso James Hill, who functions as a sort of musical uncle. As they sharpen their skills on the ukulele, members also get a chance to see the rest of the world. They've recently

◔ The Langley Ukulele Ensemble is proof that the uke isn't confined to the tropics. The group, consisting of students in middle school, high school and college, is based in Langley, British Columbia.

◔◔ Image of *Facing Future* album used with permission. Courtesy of Mountain Apple Company HAWAII / Big Boy Records. www.mountainapplecompany.com/iz

performed in Hawaii, California, Texas, Japan, Spain and the United Kingdom, with a repertoire that's international in scope and fluent in many different languages. Wherever they go, the twenty to twenty-five members speak with one eloquent voice.

A NUMBER OF great players have inevitably been omitted from the preceding list of contemporary ukeluminaries. But the most important of them all is a man or woman who isn't a great player at all.

He or she is The Ordinary Strummer.

Millions of Ordinary Strummers are scattered all over the world. Most of them are on the far side of fifty and can remember the golden age of the jukebox, the big bands and the songs of the '30s and '40s. Many play a ukulele inherited from a mother or father, or picked up for next to nothing at a flea market.

Ordinary Strummers are sometimes urged to perform, sometimes they just volunteer. They play at family gatherings, parties, celebrations and events, and occasionally with other ukists. They may or may not belong to a ukulele club, but usually not. They're very fond of their ukes, but they don't take them all that seriously.

Ordinary Strummers don't always need an event or a gathering to break out their ukes. They often play by themselves, purely for their own pleasure. They not only play but sing, if they can remember the words. Otherwise, they hum. The index finger agitates the strings, producing a gentle and friendly sound. They strum, they sing, they smile. Strum, sing, smile. Strum, sing, smile.

This song, for instance, written in the early 1930s, might serve Ordinary Strummers as a kind of ukulele anthem.

When you're smiling,
When you're smiling,
The whole world smiles with you.
When you're smiling,
When you're smiling,
The sun comes shining through.
'Cause when you're crying
You bring on the rain
So stop your sighing, be happy again.
Yes, when you're smiling,
When you're smiling,
The whole world smiles
with you.

other notable names

While Jake Shimabukuro may be called the "Jimi Hendrix of the ukulele," Canadian James Hill has been called the Wayne Gretzky of the instrument. No matter what you call him, Hill is one of the rare ukulele virtuosos who are making audiences think twice about the instrument's possibilities. Photo by Minoru Sato, courtesy James Hill.

Amanda Palmer, best known as lead singer and keyboardist for the Dresden Dolls, turned to the ukulele for her 2010 album *Amanda Palmer Performs The Popular Hits Of Radiohead On Her Magical Ukulele*. Photo by Ila Desai, courtesy Amanda Palmer.

"Ukulele Darling" Brittni Paiva is aptly nicknamed, as her native Hawaii can't seem to bestow enough honors on her. Paiva's ukulele takes on Spanish guitar songs show such levels of emotion—from tenderness to melancholy to furious celebration—as would make any Latin classicist proud. Photo by Chris Butcher, courtesy Brittni Paiva.

matchmaker, matchmaker

Putting the Ukulele Together, with Woods and with People

UKEPHORIA ATTACKS its victims in several different forms, but the most virulent is probably the making of ukuleles. That's chiefly because makers are likely to be players and collectors as well. They graduate from one stage of the virus to the next, finally mingling all three strains in a single mania.

This condition is sometimes intensified by economics. Only a sparse scattering of craftsmen manage to make ukuleles for a living, a fact that naturally stimulates their anxieties.

On the American mainland, just a very few of the makers that flourished during the 1920s and '30s still exist. Martin, then the king of the industry, today produces ukes only on special order and at prices close to stratospheric. You can often buy a vintage Martin for substantially less money than a similar contemporary model. Gibson, Martin's most formidable competitor at

◖◗ All ukuleles start out here—in a workshop full of boards. At the DaSilva Ukulele Co. in Berkeley, California, the boards combined with templates (opposite) create a yin-yang effect: would a given board make a shape you have, or do you find a board that will fit the desired shape?

the time, is now altogether out of the uke business. The other brands, hundreds of them, have vanished down Memory Lane.

In Hawaii, the pioneer makers were no less devastated. By the end of the Great Depression, most of them had closed their doors. But one has not only persevered, it has managed to prosper and expand.

Today the Kamaka brand is one of the most highly respected ukuleles in the world. Certainly it's the most widely known and consistently successful. From its beginnings in old Sam Kamaka's basement, the one-man shop became a company and is now a humming uke factory.

Kamaka has always been a family business. Old Sam passed its management along to his son Sam Jr., who in turn relinquished control to his nephew Fred a few years ago. His nephew may be running things now, but Sam has only *sort of* retired. Now in his eighties, he still shows up at the plant to conduct regular tours for present and potential customers, serving as an in-house public-relations man. Lean and energetic, with silvery hair and a wit as quick as his smile, he's very good at his job.

He commenced a recent tour with a brief review of the past. "By 1928," he said, "my father knew that the old Portuguese system was in trouble. The instruments were too shrill, the sound too thin. So he found ways to improve the system, and then he introduced a new ukulele. This was the Kamaka

A close-up of the original Kamaka Painted Pineapple uke. Photos this spread courtesy Kamaka Hawaii, Inc.

sound—fuller, richer, deeper, more romantic. It put our company on the map."

As the tour progressed, it appeared that the plant was dominated by machines rather than human hands. Kamaka quickly corrected that impression. His attitude toward technology was that of a teenager toward a grandparent—dutiful but perfunctory. "We've got the best engineering here that money can buy," he said. "But there are some things a machine just can't do." He gestured toward a person masked to protect his lungs against the dust produced by whirring lathes and saws. "Look over there," he said, and then pointed toward another gloved and hooded worker with a blowtorch. "Or look over there. For really important stuff, we still rely on people. Always have. Always will."

In the past, when his father was in charge, about half of the company's workers were hard of hearing. "It's a pretty common belief that the deaf have a special sensitivity to sound," Kamaka explained. "They may not be able to hear the sound, but the theory is that they can feel the vibrations through their fingertips. This makes it possible for them to judge the quality of the wood in ways that normal people can't. Is it true?" He shrugged, "Well, my dad never denied it."

Until then, any mention of his father had been reverential. Now his tone sharpened.

"Those deaf workers were grateful for any kind of a job," he continued. "Never complained, never called in sick, never asked for a raise. They were easy to push around. That was the main reason why my

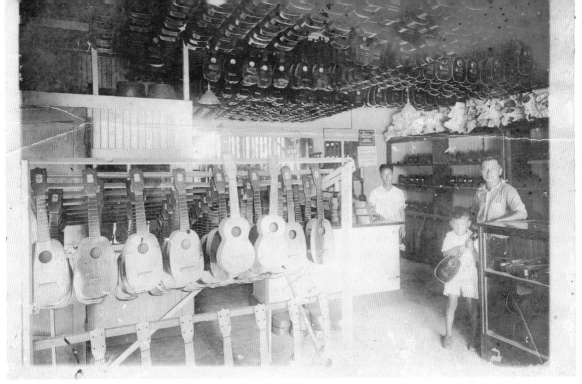

↑ Sam Kamaka Sr. and his son, Fred, in the original Kamaka factory.

↓ In 1959, Kamaka & Sons expanded and moved to its current location on South Street in Honolulu.

father hired them. He was not what you'd call a sympathetic man."

Once he acknowledged that his father was not without defects, Kamaka proceeded to develop the theme of imperfection.

"I went to work in the factory when I was ten years old," he said. "Swept the floor, ran errands—stuff like that. I also learned a little about the making of ukuleles. My father was a tyrant, and his teaching methods were cruel. To get even, my brother and I wasted wood—on purpose. To ukulele makers, wood is more precious than gold. We used to drive the old man nuts."

Kamaka went on with his recollections. "I wasn't much interested in the ukulele until I was in high school. Then I began to notice girls, and that changed things. I thought that a uke might help get me their attention. 'Give me a uke,' I kept nagging. 'Dad, give me a uke.' Dad refused. Said I'd have to earn one. So, with his help, I learned how to put a uke together. It wasn't easy, but I wound up with something to strum for the girls."

Sam Jr. was more or less expected to enter the family business when he graduated from high school, but he had other ideas. His father was too exacting a taskmaster to make that prospect very appealing. Instead, he enlisted in the Army, where the disciplines were actually more relaxed than at the plant. He remained a soldier for almost twenty years. Only when his father was finally getting ready to step aside did he leave the service and begin his second career as a ukulele maker.

↑ The headstock of a Pineapple ukulele from the 1930s.

↶ Sam Kamaka Jr., holding a Pineapple ukulele. Photos this spread courtesy Kamaka Hawaii, Inc.

Times had changed, but not his father. "With Dad," he said, "it was his way or no way. What he said, went. He liked new ideas, all right, so long as they were *his* ideas. And he had a lot of good ones. He changed the voice of the ukulele. He changed its shape—created a very famous uke that looked like a pineapple. He helped changed the way that people think and feel about the ukulele. But he never ever changed himself. Sam Kamaka Sr. always stayed the same."

The changes that Sam Jr. introduced during his run as head of the company were mostly technological. The dangerous and laborious work that used to be done by hand was now assigned to automated machines. "Nobody gets burned or cut the way they once did," Kamaka said. "The whole process is much safer and more efficient." He jerked a thumb toward a massive piece of equipment that stood at the heart of the assembly line. "See that machine? It'll do stuff you just can't believe. Kind of sensitive, though. When it gets temperamental, we have to import a specialist all the way from Germany to put it back in shape. Nobody here in Hawaii can really figure it out."

Today the Kamaka ukulele business employs some thirty full-time workers and produces between four thousand and five thousand instruments a year. "Depends to some extent on the weather," Kamaka said ruefully. "When we get really heavy rains, the moisture in the air slows down our sanding and finishing work."

The company makes soprano, tenor and baritone ukuleles, all on order. Custom refinements are handled by an independent department. These cosmetics and embroideries, not any enhancement of sound quality, fetch higher prices. "Our ukuleles used to be solid koa, top to bottom," Kamaka said. "Now we make them with mahogany necks."

The instruments displayed in the reception area are not for sale. Customers are warned that they'll have to wait a month for the delivery of a single uke, and even longer for volume sales to retailers. A couple of years ago, the company agreed to produce one hundred signature ukuleles for Jake Shimabukuro, who in turn sells them at fancy prices to his infatuated fans. "Got us into hot water," Kamaka remembered. "Jammed up the whole production schedule. Couldn't satisfy the demand, and couldn't hire additional help because we just didn't have enough space."

The space problem may be solved in a year or so. The company's present two-story building is located in an area that's due to be reclaimed by the City of Honolulu. Plans are already in the works for a move to more spacious quarters. "That'll give us a chance to expand," Sam Jr. said. "We're thinking about some new products. And we have to make sure that we continue to develop our sales in Japan. We're already selling about 25 percent of our ukuleles to the Japanese. It's a huge market. Insatiable, it seems."

Another benefit of the company's move could be an improved security system. "Sure hope so," Kamaka said. "We're besieged by wood pirates. Can't keep 'em out. We've tried just about everything—electrified fences, alarms, spotlights, video surveillance. Nothing seems to work very well. They still get away with our seasoned koa by the truckload. If we could cut our security and insurance costs by one-half, you'd be able to get a Kamaka ukulele for a lot less than you pay right now."

Sam Jr. is content to surrender command of the company to his nephew. "Fred doesn't talk as much as I do," he said, "but he's a very good businessman. Has to be, these days."

Among the least of Kamaka's concerns are the thirty or so other ukulele makers now operating in Hawaii. "Excellent craftsmen," he allowed. "Not so hot at the business details, though. To my way of thinking, we only have one real competitor. That's Martin, and they don't actually manufacture a regular line of ukuleles any more. They have the skills and the capacity, but their business now is the guitar."

Kamaka ukuleles are featured in many Hawaiian school programs. Some schools own over one hundred Kamakas. Tours of kids often troop through the plant, thirty at a time. "Have to keep a sharp eye on them," Kamaka said, "especially with so many razor-edged machines in operation. In the old days, the Hawaiian kids could be real roughnecks. They used the ukes as clubs and left them in splinters."

Toward the end of the tour, Kamaka spoke briefly of what the ukulele has meant to his family. "I have six girls and four boys," he said. "Two of them are airline pilots. Another is a lawyer, another a doctor, still another the comptroller of a very successful business. Everybody's doing well." He smiled. "Without the ukulele, none of all that might have happened. The uke has been very, very good to all of us."

WHEN SOMEONE evicts his cars from the garage and parks them to gradually weather and rust in the street, you can be pretty sure that the evacuated space is being used for another purpose. It might become an extra bedroom, or a darkroom, or a laundry room, or just a place to stow the unending acquisition of possessions that the owner can't bear to give or throw away.

↻ Mike DaSilva at the control center of the workshop: his workbench.

↻ Up on a shelf are the forms and clamps used to create the walls of the ukulele soundbox. Like the lasts a shoemaker uses, these seem to be marked with a particular customer's name.

He found it in music. During this period, usually by himself, he'd been picking a bluegrass banjo. He even built a banjo, following the directions furnished by a how-to kit. "Taught me a lot," DaSilva says. "I began to understand something about how instruments really work, and also something about the physics of sound."

At the same time, DaSilva made another significant decision. He bought himself a ukulele.

Mike DaSilva's garage, for instance, became a ukulele laboratory.

At first DaSilva created instruments simply for his own satisfaction. Now, just as old Sam Kamaka did back in 1916, he operates his own one-man ukulele business.

The ukulele originated in Portugal, and passionate Portuguese blood flows in DaSilva's veins. A trim and vigorous man, his rich olive skin, alert dark dyes and dainty goatee give him the swashbuckling look of a Mediterranean adventurer.

His career has certainly demonstrated that he's not averse to risk. He originally intended to become a chemical engineer but dropped out of college to study the almost infinite possibilities of the computer. Before he was thirty, he was heading a multi-million dollar lab for a billion dollar startup company. Then he went out on his own as a freelance programmer, earning up to $1,500 a day. The work was rewarding, but DaSilva still hungered for another kind of fulfillment.

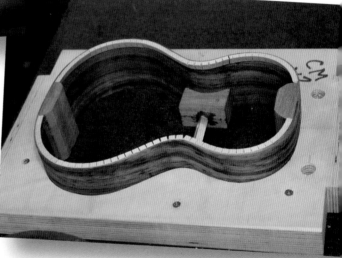

"It was a beat-up old 1920 Martin," he recalls. "My family banned the banjo, but they tolerated the uke. They didn't know that it would become a kind of obsession to me. First I bought a couple of instruction books and did a lot of serious practicing. Then, since I had some disposable income in those days, I began to build a uke collection. But it was when I attended a festival in New Jersey that I really became a believer. That was an experience. It was like something out of *Close Encounters of the Third Kind*—I simply had to go. I felt very funny about it. My wife kept giving me weird looks, as though I was looney tunes. Maybe I was, in a way. We're not married anymore."

He didn't say why. The divorce may or may not have been caused by his preoccupation with the ukulele.

"Anyhow," he continued, "I had a great time there in New Jersey. About two hundred people showed up. All of them had been bitten by the uke bug, big time. John King, the ukulele classicist, was there. And an amateur maker brought along the first two ukes that came out of his workshop. He gave me some important insights on how to get started. The whole event was sort of like a revival meeting. By the time it was over, I was totally converted. I found a place for myself. I felt I belonged."

Back in California, DaSilva put his career as a computer programmer on hold. Then he parked the family cars in the driveway and turned his garage into a ukulele lab.

- Mike selects a thin sheet of koa wood for the soundbox walls.
- The wall material is cut and bent into the form, then clamped.
- The soundbox is then brought to the bench where the back and soundboard are attached.

"My plan was to play the market in the morning and make ukuleles in the afternoon," DaSilva said. "That scheme didn't last very long. Pretty soon I was working full time on the ukes and living off my savings. I did a lot of preliminary research—woods, glues, lacquers, designs, everything. Then I managed to acquire a vintage Martin 3K—one of the finest ukuleles Martin or anyone else ever turned out. Ever since then, I've tested my own instruments against that model—again and again, chord after chord, note after note. And in the process, little by little, I taught myself to listen. Listening is a gift, but also a skill. After awhile, I learned to really hear those undertones and overtones, the subtle shadings and echoes of sound."

What he came to understand, DaSilva explained, was that every ukulele has its own natural voice. "They're like human beings in that way," he said. "The qualities of the wood, not the abilities of the maker, determines its character. When I make a ukulele, I don't feel that I'm its master. I just help it speak for itself. If I were in complete control, the mystery and the meaning of what I try to do might be lost."

In 2004, the Santa Cruz Ukulele Club staged its Ukefest West. DaSilva was among the eight hundred avid ukemaniacs to attend. With him he brought six ukuleles—the first he'd ever exposed to the public. At the event he met an old friend, Mark Gutierrez. A knowledgeable judge of ukuleles, Gutierrez tested one of DaSilva's inventory and bought it on the spot. "That convinced me," DaSilva said. "The next day, I paid $50 for a vendor's table and put my remaining five ukes up for sale. By the end of the event, not one of them was left. 'Hey,' I said to myself, 'maybe I'm onto something here.' So I went home and set myself up in business."

By now his garage was just about exploding with wood and tools. "I had to construct little tunnels to get from here to there," he recalls. He then sublet a 1,200-square-foot studio, which he just about filled with sawdust in six months. His landlord, not quite certain of DaSilva's sanity, told him to move. When he did, it was into his present work space in Berkeley, California.

The shop is located among a nest of studios occupied by artisans and craftsmen of all kinds. DaSilva's is one of the biggest—a single sky-lighted room of 2,500 square feet. Woods of different types are carefully stacked along the walls. The forklift that DaSilva uses to hoist and handle the lumber stands off to one side. "When we got divorced," he said wryly, "my wife got the house. I got the forklift." Workbenches and production machinery occupy about two-thirds of the space. The remaining area contains a sofa, a few chairs, and an elevated stage that's festooned with sound equipment.

DaSilva is still a one-man operation. Most of his instruments are sopranos, but he makes tenors and baritones as well. They range in price from $600 up to $3,000 apiece. He has a tough time keeping pace with his orders. His customers are obliged to wait

The finished soundbox is given time to dry.

Decorative edging is added.

The necks are made from different types of wood.

Once the neck has been roughed out, the rest requires plenty of elbow grease and a wood file.

eight to twelve weeks for delivery. Well over a hundred DaSilva ukuleles are now in circulation.

DaSilva's methods and techniques are more sophisticated than those of the early Portuguese pioneers, but in essence they remain very much the surfaces. The sinuous contours of the ukulele, which follow the natural patterns of the grain, are seductively appealing to him. "Once spent three months helping to build a yacht," he said. "Had a wonderful time. Not a straight piece of wood in the whole vessel."

Kamaka ukuleles are mostly koa, with mahogany necks. DaSilva is less rigid. He uses an assortment of koa, fir, and three different species of spruce. The decisions depend on the tone desired by the customer, which is identified in preliminary interviews.

same. "I make the bottoms and tops first," he said, "then the sides. The sides are shaped under extreme heat. Then comes the neck, rasped by hand to snuggle in the player's palm. It's not just filed. It's sculpted." He paused, savoring the word. "I've always liked to work with my hands," he said.

His hands are DaSilva's most valuable tools, but he has his doubts about the stone-deaf workers who are believed to feel the currents of sound in wood. "I think it's a myth," he said. "Nobody can really feel those vibrations. Weight and thickness—yes. I can measure those very exactly—with my eyes closed or blindfolded. Many of my most critical judgments are based on what I learn through my hands. When a uke turns out to be something special, I usually know before I ever strike a note."

DaSilva loves wood as a painter loves color. He prefers working with curved shapes and

form an idea of the ukulele they want—soft and gentle, sharp and aggressive, whatever. This makes it possible for me to fashion an instrument that fits them like a hand-tailored suit made to measure. In any case the project should be a collaboration between me and the customer. If it isn't, I'm always doubtful about the results."

Until recently, DaSilva was producing only six ukuleles per month. "Not enough," he said. "Had to improve my numbers." Now he's turning out about ten a month—up 40 percent. "I'm making progress," he said, "but I still have a way to go. Neither I nor anyone else will ever match what one great maker accomplished over in Hawaii. He made five thousand ukes before he died, all by himself, all by hand. And believe it

← **The finished product.**

→ **Having finished one ukulele, and about to finish another, Mike is pretty pleased with his products.**

or not, that guy had a regular day job. He was a uke maker only on the side."

These sessions are essential to DaSilva's philosophy. He considers himself not only a ukemaker but a matchmaker. He prepares a union between the customer and the instrument with intensive questioning and analysis.

"Above all," he said, "I help them to listen. It's the same process I apply to myself. I look for exact and truthful descriptions of sound. We use three different ukuleles—three different voices. Then I ask the customers to compare them, to judge them, to tell me what they like and what they don't. I insist that they use factual straightforward language—no jargon, no vague mushy poetics. From these interviews I can

From the initial selection of the wood to the final mounting of the strings, a DaSilva ukulele is created in fifteen different stages. It's cut, molded and bent under extreme heat. It's rasped and sanded, rasped and sanded, rasped and sanded. "More of the wood ends up as sawdust," DaSilva said, "than is left in the completed instrument." Much of the required equipment is partly or entirely made by DaSilva himself. Then, by hand, the ukulele is fitted and glued together. The neck is shaped and attached. Then the finishing ritual begins. DaSilva no longer coats his ukulele with lacquer. He treats it with polyester, instead, which is naturally cured by the light.

He picked up a nearly completed ukulele, embracing the neck with his fingers. "It should nestle in the palm," he said. "The hand should act as a cradle."

DaSilva is more than just a ukulele maker. He's a tireless ukulele advocate. He advances the cause of the instrument however and whenever he can. A few years ago he founded the Berkeley Ukulele Club, and it now has about fifty regular and irregular members. They meet once a month in DaSilva's studio. Some are novices, some accomplished performers. As ukulele beginners and proficients usually do, they get along very well together. The meetings combine tutorials, demonstrations, individual recitals and impromptu strum-alongs. DaSilva provides the premises, keeps the minutes, writes the newsletter, and serves as the general caretaker.

On top of that, he also organizes and promotes occasional concerts by local and visiting uke luminaries. That's why he's constructed the stage and sound system that occupy part of his workplace. It's sometimes used as a recording studio too. A number of albums and CDs have been produced on the premises, and more are in the works.

"I'm thinking hard about associated business possibilities," DaSilva said. "I could keep afloat the way I'm going, but I can't save any money. It's pretty much a break-even proposition. The cost of wood, of course, is always a concern. I cut a good deal for a considerable supply back when I first got started, but the price keeps going up, up, up. To expand, I probably have to take on a well-heeled partner. Well, we'll see. I'm pretty busy right now, making my best ukulele yet."

He smiled.

"The best ukulele," he said, "is always the next ukulele."

OF THE SEVERAL HUNDRED ukulele makers in the United States today, only fifty or so are true professionals. The rest are ardent amateurs of widely differing skill and experience, laboring alone in makeshift workshops without business licenses.

At the head of the pros stands Kamaka Hawaii Incorporated. No other maker produces so many ukuleles of such distinguished quality. Next in line, at least in terms of business know-how and number of instruments sold, probably comes the Magic Fluke Company of Connecticut, which is part of impresario Jim Beloff's empire of ukulele interests. Most of the others, like Mike DaSilva's company, are very small or one-man operations. Struggling to establish a niche in the market, they often specialize in this or that particular type of uke—electronic, reproductions and replicas of

classic models, six and eight-string ukuleles, metal and reso-phonic ukes. One maker even offers construction lessons to inspiring beginners.

Almost no maker, big or small, has the guts or the resources to speculate on ukulele production. Not until they receive an order and also some kind of payment in advance do they pick up their tools. Kamaka Hawaii Incorporated sells in volume to retailers, DaSilva only to individuals. But both operate on the same principal. The money must be committed before the work begins.

Most purchasers, of course, don't deal directly with the makers. Why should they? They just go to the music store, where they select an instrument out of inventory on the urging of a salesperson who may know as much about the ukuleles as about rocket science.

Yet some seekers want something different, something better, something distinctly their own. So off they go to a maker as they might to a portrait painter. "Create me a ukulele," they say. "My voice. My personality. You know—*me*."

How and where to find the right uke maker isn't always easy. It's a little like trying to find the right doctor or auto mechanic. Makers rarely advertise. They depend for the most part on the recommendations of satisfied customers. You therefore seek the counsel of other ukulele enthusiasts, who suggest this name or that name. You consult web sites, write emails, make phone calls. You may even fly to Hawaii, ostensibly on vacation—but while you're there, just by chance, you may drop in on a maker whose name has been mentioned by a player you especially respect. The trade winds murmur and the surf thunders, but you remain in a sunless workshop until you finally make your decision.

But wait a minute. There's that other guy, also highly praised, in Finland or Thailand or Australia or Argentina or Japan. Maybe you should check him out before you write a check.

The makers, wherever and whoever they are, sigh and patiently wait.

They understand. They've been bitten by the same bug.

I Found a million Dollar Baby (In a Five and Ten Cent Store)

The Craze of Collecting

For mysterious reasons they themselves may never understand, many otherwise rational people become collectors. Avidly and obsessively, they collect coins, postage stamps, Barbie dolls, Elvis Presley memorabilia, baseball cards, first editions, comic books, porcelains and pottery, quilts and needlework. The wealthy collect works of art, vintage automobiles, rare wines, vacation houses and divorces. The less fortunate collect foreclosure notes, food stamps and unemployment insurance. Reclusive widows collect cats. Entomologists collect dead butterflies.

Many of us are collectors of another kind. We collect junk.

Because we possess so much and throw away so little, our attics

⟲ ⟳ **Sandor Nagyszalanczy has been collecting ukuleles for many years. He has amassed a collection of nearly four hundred of them.**

groan under the weight of ancient *National Geographics*, musty and outdated clothing, obsolete television sets and radio consoles, decrepit pianos, rust-bitten golf clubs, abandoned exercise equipment, outdated Encyclopedia Britannicas, and boxes upon boxes of yellowing family history. When we run out of space, we cram the overflow into rented storage units. "The kids will want to have this one day," we insist, unable to admit that they probably won't have the slightest interest in any of it. Neither will anyone else. Nevertheless, we continue to acquire, to accumulate, to collect.

Even among the most extreme of collectors, ukists are uncommonly passionate. They pursue their acquisitions with a quivering intensity of bloodhounds after possum. Some enthusiasts will travel around the world to negotiate the purchase of an especially rare and precious instrument. Marriages have floundered and failed because husbands are more devoted to their ukuleles than to their indignant wives.

Sandor Nagyszalanczy is not a collector of this type. He's retained his sanity and has achieved a balanced understanding with his wife about the importance of his collection.

He was born in Hungary, is descended from aristocrats of that vanished kingdom, and immigrated to the United States with his family when he was two and a half. "My father was a brilliant engineer," he says, "but too impatient to ever fix anything around the house. I learned pretty early to be good with my hands."

By the time he enrolled in college, Sandor had already commenced his ardent affair with the ukulele. It was a Martin, given to him as a gift from his then girlfriend. She purchased the uke for $1 in a thrift store in California's central valley. He majored in environmental planning and design, but when he graduated he decided to be a furniture designer/craftsman instead. "I was too impatient to spend years at school getting a degree in architecture. Woodworking seemed like it would be a lot more fun."

Then he opened a custom furniture business in Santa Cruz, which did well enough to help him pay for the ukuleles he was beginning to collect. His mother, who'd become a buyer of fine antiques for well-heeled clients, approved of Sandor's collecting and often helped him out. Her discerning eye occasionally detected likely ukuleles in out-of-the-way junk shops. One of them, a vintage Martin 5K, the holy grail of ukes, which she obtained for $125, was presented to Sandor as an incentive. "Collect on," his mother instructed.

"I did collect on," Sandor says.

Before long, he made a slight detour in his career, moved to the east coast and started writing and editing articles for a woodworking journal. Typically spending a week a month on the road visiting authors and taking photos, Sandor scoured local shops for instruments after his assignments were complete. "The uke was an almost forgotten instrument in those days. You could still pick up real bargains. Like most collectors, I spent a lot of time in antique shops and flea markets, always on the prowl for undervalued treasures." One pilgrimage took Sandor to the Martin guitar and ukulele factory in Pennsylvania. There he spent many hours talking ukulele with Martin's resident historian and uke fancier Mike Longworth. "He'd been researching the history of Martin instruments for decades and shared many tales of the colorful past of the ukulele." Sandor recalls. "For example, Mike told me about how mysterious the various woods used in ukuleles could be. Three ukes made from the same tree to exactly the same specs, he told me, can sound very different. One could be lousy, one pretty good, and the third

terrific. And then he explained it in a way I'll always remember. 'It might depend on which side of the tree the ukes were made out of that some pygmy decided to piss on.'" Sometime earlier, Sandor had joined a quartet of singers who whimsically called themselves The JeloTones. "We did jungle arrangements," he says. "You know—doo-wop numbers. For some songs, I'd pull out my uke, which I kept conveniently tucked into the back of my belt. Lots of fun. And we kept pretty busy—private parties, special events of one kind or another. Spent twenty years with the JeloTones, collecting all the time."

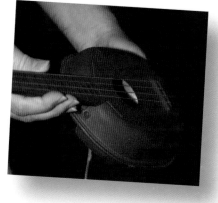

Toward the end of this period, Sandor was approached by a couple of fellow enthusiasts who were forming a ukulele club in Santa Cruz. He thought it a pretty good idea and agreed to become an officer. "I'm the club's dedicated TechMeister," he says. At meetings, I try to provide entertaining information and advice about the instrument itself—history, construction, care and maintenance, all that stuff. I can make ukuleles, you know. I have the skills and some experience. But I'm essentially a collector, not a maker. Those other guys create ukes. I appreciate them."

While building his ukulele collection, Sandor also built his reputation as one of the country's leading authorities on woodworking. He's authored well over a hundred articles on the subject, along with more than a dozen distinctive books on tools and techniques, all illustrated by handsome photographs taken by himself. He's an accomplished photographer whose images are also sought by publishers of works that have little or nothing to do with woodworking.

Sandor welcomes these assignments and is ready to explore new possibilities.

Sandor lives today in the redwood-forested mountains that overlook Santa Cruz. One wing of his home is dedicated to his ukulele collection. He now owns nearly four hundred ukes, which he sometimes loans to museums for exhibition. Some are rare and very valuable antiques. Others are less venerable but distinguished by their exceptional quality of tone and craftsmanship. Many more are novelties of the kind so prolifically manufactured in the 1920s and '30s, and his collection of plastic instruments is among the most extensive in the country.

It was on one of his visits with friends at Martin that Sandor was told about a nearly forgotten cache of vintage plastic guitars and possibly ukuleles gathering dust in a warehouse just north of New York City. He was electrified by the news. These weren't just anybody's instruments. They'd been made by Mario Maccaferri, the most celebrated pioneer of plastic instruments. How and why that happened is a story in itself (see sidebar, opposite).

The worth of Sandor's entire collection is difficult to calculate, but he's confident that he'd realize a handsome profit if he put it up for sale. That's something he isn't anxious to do. "Don't even think about it much," he says. "I'm fond of the instruments, and I don't need the money."

Sooner or later, however, all important collectors are forced to ask themselves the same insistent questions. What am I eventually going to do with what I've put together? Should I sell it piece by piece or as a group? In fact, should I sell it at all? Would it be better to bequeath my collection to a museum, or

wood you like paper or plastic?

UNTIL THE 1930s, almost all ukuleles were made of wood and crafted for the most part by hand. Wood doesn't yield easily to mass production. It's too temperamental, too individualistic. It's also very expensive.

After World War II, however, synthetic materials began to infiltrate ukulele production. Nylon, Bakelite and Styrene, to cite just three, could be molded into any shape, and could also transmit the necessary vibrations. This enabled manufacturers to simplify their methods and eliminate many costly and time-consuming steps. Seeking increased speed and economy, these heretics started to produce ukuleles composed partly or wholly of plastic.

Musically, the results were often lamentable. The price was sharply reduced, but so was the quality of the sound. Ukulele purists denounced the plastic cheapies as the work of the devil.

But over in Europe a gifted engineer named Mario Maccaferri had already proved that instruments of exceptional quality could be created with synthetics. He'd built his reputation on plastic reeds for clarinets and saxophones and had also designed special jazz guitars for Selmer that were used by the gypsy genius Django Reinhardt. Now he was ready to invest his skill, experience and money in an effort to produce plastic ukes.

When he first came to the United States, Maccaferri's intention was to create a musical toy priced at about $5. Then his conscience got the better of him. He decided to pursue a nobler goal—the best plastic guitars and ukuleles his hands and mind could contrive. First he worked out a deal with Dow Chemical, which supplied financial and engineering support. He put up $75,000 of his own money. Five U.S. patents and many months later, he finally achieved an instrument that satisfied his requirements.

⬆ **The Chord Master was an optional add-on to the Islander ukulele. The Chord Master could be attached to the neck and would automatically create chords with the push of a button.**

The Islander, as Maccaferri christened it, became the Strad of plastic ukes. It was introduced and assiduously promoted by Arthur Godfrey on his various TV programs. Nobody could hustle a product more artfully than the old redhead. At one point in 1950, Maccaferri's company in New York was churning out a reported 1,500 ukes a day, with a waiting list of 100,000 orders backed up.

The Islander was originally priced at $5.95, which was later whittled to $3.95. The production cost was $1.50 each, on which Maccaferri realized twenty-five cents. But the bonanza didn't last forever. The company closed its doors in the late 1960s. The Islander and other Maccaferri products—a baritone ukulele, a ukette for kids, a patented Visual Chord Master—are all avidly sought by collectors. Almost no maker today continues to produce plastic ukuleles.

even to create some kind of a foundation to serve as a permanent home? What's best for the collection? What's best for me?

Sandor has occasionally discussed this issue with his friend and fellow officer of the Santa Cruz Ukulele Club, Andy Andrews, who's assembled a formidable collection of his own. They share the same concerns, and the same instinct to go slow. There's been some preliminary talk about what to do with the collections, but no action so far.

These days, Sandor continues to collect, though at a much more deliberate pace than before. "The bargains are no longer there," he says. "Anyway, I'm running out of space. I don't think we'd like to build an addition to the house for even more ukuleles. There always comes a time when you have to say enough is enough."

SANDOR'S COLLECTION is very important but by no means unique. Others are scattered all over the country. You can find them in many American cities, and sometimes in small towns and villages as well. You can never be sure where a uke collector is going to turn up.

Probably the most comprehensive ukulele collection in the world belongs to a Japanese enthusiast. He doesn't build his inventory instrument by instrument. He collects collections. It was this connoisseur who acquired the vast ukulele properties of Chuck Fayne, an American then living in Australia, thereby multiplying his already immense ukulele collection in Japan. These days, it seems, ukulele investments can be swapped back and forth like international hedge funds.

Now that collectible ukuleles have become so painfully expensive, enthusiasts on limited budgets must satisfy themselves on leavings and leftovers of ukulele collections. They prospect for nuggets of period sheet music, of vintage songbooks, of toys, of ukulele gimmicks and thingamajigs of all kinds. Objects once scorned as oddball trivialities now adorn mantelpieces and are cherished in display cabinets. One collector, a shadowy character who bills himself as "Ukulele Ray" actually turned his home in Southern California into a sort of shrine for such exotica. Ray is not his real name, which for reasons of his own he rarely reveals. (It's rumored that he was once a porn star.) Unfortunately, the shrine he created no longer exists. He's reported to have recently sold most of his collection and is said to be living somewhere in Arizona.

NO LIST of the world's most zealous and dedicated collectors can omit a man whose goals and methods may have been unique.

John King was probably the greatest interpreter of classical works ever attempted on the ukulele. While other virtuosos played the songs of Irving Berlin, King rendered the compositions of Johann Sebastian Bach. He could strum along with the best of them on less lofty materials, but his compelling passion was for the formalities of the distant past. His studies rescued the obscure scores of many works from neglect and oblivion.

Though King owned his share of distinguished ukuleles, he wasn't really a collector of instruments. He collected knowledge instead. King was generally considered to be the most learned of ukulele historians. Nobody knew more about how, when, where or why the ukulele evolved than this scholar. Fellow authorities often sought his counsel and guidance, deferring to his judgments as though to an oracle.

↑ **Another fine memento from Sandor's collection.**

King's reputation and influence was and is based chiefly on his book, *The Hawaiian Ukulele and Guitar Makers*, which was published in 2001. Meticulously researched, it accepts no romantic myths or alluring speculations about the uke. King was revered for his mild and accommodating temperament, but his insistence on the accurate treatment of facts was implacable. Nor was he a man to be rushed. He'd been working for years on an even more exhaustive and ambitious history of the ukulele—a labor he'll never be able to complete.

Suddenly and far too soon, John King died of a heart attack while the last chapters of this book were being written. He was 54 years old. Perhaps another scholar can be found to finish the work he'd intended. If that scholar measures up to the standards that John King established for himself, the book will surely become a ukulele bible.

John King is gone now. If indeed there are angels in heaven, they're probably playing their harps, but the newcomer will be playing his ukulele.

Farewell, John King. Strum in peace.

HAWAIIAN
Aloha!
BEYOND THE REEF
BLUE HAWAII
LOVELY HULA HANDS
PEARLY SHELLS
JIM'S
UKULELE beach party
26 Songs about the sea and the swingin' scene on the shore... arranged for UKULELE
Compiled and Arranged by JIM BELOFF
HAPPY TOGETHER
ALL MY LOVING
DAYDREAM
SURFER GIRL
Jumpin' Jim's
UKULELE MASTERS
LYLE RITZ
CD Included
SOLOS
15 Chord Solos
Ukulele Jazz Master
The UKULELE
A Visual History
REVISED & EXPANDED
CRAZY WORDS CRAZY TUNE
VO-DO-DE-O
HERB OHTA

There's no Business Like Uke Business

The Ins and Outs of the Ukulele Trade

MILLIONS OF PEOPLE TODAY play, collect or make ukuleles. But only a microscopic few manage to scratch out a living with the ukulele alone.

Many virtuosos are obliged to play the guitar or the bass for their bread and butter. Collectors rarely profit, either. Most are reluctant to put their four-stringed darlings on the market. Even most of the makers in the world aren't really in it for the money. Worldwide, perhaps fifty do well and another hundred or so limp along. Meantime, at night and on weekends, the majority labor in their basements and garages for the sheer joy of the craft.

Jim Beloff, however, confounds all these stereotypes.

Beloff is a unique one-man ukulele industry—a player and performer, a songwriter, a historian and archivist, a collector, a publisher, a manufacturer, a merchant and an indefatigable promoter who's converted his passion for the uke into an improbably successful business.

"One-man ukulele industry," though, is a description that might make Beloff wince with discomfort. He's a dedicated family man, and his company, Flea Market Music, is very much a family operation. Beloff's wife, Liz, a graphic designer, conceives most of the advertising and promotional materials. His brother-in-law is a gifted engineer who forms and fashions the instruments that come off the Flea Market production line. "I didn't originate the company all by myself," Beloff insists, "and I don't run it all by myself." But despite his protests, Beloff is perceived throughout ukeland as its most ubiquitous and influential single impresario.

Beloff was a New England preppie. He first picked up the guitar when he was twelve and the kids of the country were throbbing along with the beat. He and his guitar went to Hampshire College, a high-toned experimental school. There Beloff experimented in songwriting and the study of musical theatre.

During a summer break, Beloff spent four months in New York. He was hoping to finagle a job

◐ **Jim Beloff's Flea Market Music has created a ukulele empire, publishing and recording the greats of the past, and present, and making some darn good ukes too.**

125

in the theater—"pushing a broom," he said, "any kind of a job." His school counselors told him to approach the producers of off-Broadway musicals, but Beloff has never been timid. "I didn't contact anybody but the best," he said. "I wrote to Stephen Sondheim. I wrote to Leonard Bernstein. And you know what happened? I wound up working with them both—Allen J. Lerner, too."

After he graduated, Beloff returned to New York and resumed his search for a career in musical theater. "While I sent out résumés," he said, "I did anything I could to keep going. I washed dishes, waited tables. Some possibilities developed, but no paychecks. I finally had to take a regular job. I was disappointed at the time, but it turned out to be a great opportunity."

The job he landed was with Ziff-Davis, the country's leading publisher of specialty magazines. "Yachting, bodybuilding, money management, cooking—you name it," Beloff said. "Ziff-Davis covered them all. My assignment involved sales, marketing and advertising. It couldn't have given me a better education to form the specialty business we operate today."

Beloff spent about ten years with Ziff-Davis, earning but also learning. He busily wrote songs, reviews and cabaret acts. And during this time he met Liz, now his wife.

A lot of the work Liz was doing was commissioned by film producers—titles, trailers, logos and so on. In 1991 they decided to pack up and head for Los Angeles, the capital of all such business, where Beloff became a West Coast executive for Ziff-Davis. But just before they left New York, at a family gathering, Beloff's father-in-law spotted a battered old uke in the shadows of the house. He'd played the ukulele as a Sea Bee during World War II. After he'd tuned it up and strummed a couple of chords, he handed it to Beloff. "Here," he said. "See what you can do with this."

Beloff's ever-present smile widened at the memory.

"I'd never given the uke a thought until that moment," he said. "It was kismet—like Fred Astaire's first dance routine with Ginger Rogers. I was stunned by the advanced chords you could create on the uke. Because you so often play all four strings at the same time, the uke becomes a chord machine. And its voice! Very different from the guitar. Warmer, gentler—a natural partner for the kind of music I love and the songs I write. Old-fashioned, some people might say. Not me. I think it's timeless."

In Los Angeles, Beloff and Liz spent a lot of their leisure hours rummaging around the Rose Bowl Flea Market looking for bargains in ukuleles, sheet music, and vintage visual materials of all kinds.

"That was in 1991 and 1992," Beloff said. "The uke was having another one of its recessions. You could pick up a pretty good Martin for $100 or so on any given day. There were almost no ukulele songbooks available in those days, either. Just a few collections by Cliff Edwards, mostly out of print. I discovered a whole stack of them at a dingy little shop in East Los Angeles and bought every one. That got me to thinking—*seriously* thinking—about the ukulele as a specialty business."

Beloff's voice became more intense.

"I don't know exactly why," he went on, "but I was sure the uke would make a comeback. And when it did, my hunch was that the world would want some ukulele songbooks. So Liz and I decided to roll the dice on a 'Jumpin' Jim' entry called *Ukulele Favorites*."

The Beloffs got some valuable help at this beginning of their ukulele enterprise. On a business trip to New York, Beloff met with a legendary songbook editor named Ronny Schiff. She steered Beloff to a

jim
beloff

sympathetic publisher, Hal Leonard, who offered Beloff a contract. That first book sold well enough to encourage a second—*Jumpin' Jim's Tips 'N' Tunes*, which did even better and is currently in its thirty-sixth printing.

"By now, in the mid 1990s, I was in a dilemma," Beloff said. "I was working for *Billboard* by this time, strictly on show business stuff. I liked the job a lot, but I was itching to see what could be done with the uke. Could I make a living with it? I wasn't sure, so I kept very busy on the side. Liz and I did a series of follow-up books. And I started work on a visual history of the ukulele—a pretty formidable job. Nothing like it had ever been published before."

The first edition of Beloff's lavishly and lovingly illustrated visual history came off the presses in 1997. Beloff had hoped to pry an introduction out of George Harrison, the retired, if not retiring, Beatle whose affection for the ukulele was widely known. Harrison, in fact, maintained a supply of extra ukes to distribute among his guests at get-togethers and dinner parties.

The negotiations with Harrison sputtered and finally stalled, but not long after his book was published Beloff received an unexpected phone call. On the line was a friend who also happened to be a pal of Harrison's. "George is in town," he told Beloff. "He likes your book, and he'd like to pay you a visit. This afternoon okay with you?"

"I was flat-out delirious," Beloff recalled. "One of the Beatles, inviting himself to drop in on *me*."

When George arrived, he turned out to be a real hambone. "As soon as he entered the house, he picked up a banjo uke and broke into one of George Formby's signature music hall favorites, 'Leaning on the Lamp Post.' I knew it, of course, and we played together for most of the afternoon, one great old tune after another. What a day! I'll never forget it. And that Christmas, George ordered a whole raft of my visual histories."

It was just about then that the Beloffs took a deep breath and decided to make Flea Market Music their career rather than just an enthusiasm. "It was a gamble," Beloff said. "The uke was still in the doldrums. Arthur Godfrey was no longer around, and Tiny Tim had become an almost grotesque caricature. Liz and I didn't exactly invent the uke as a specialty market, but we worked our butts off to keep it alive, to make it grow."

First, they continued to expand their catalogue of publications. The books were accompanied by assorted CDs and DVDs. They introduced a line of ukulele merchandise. Then they began to manufacture their own instruments—the Fluke and its smaller cousin, the Flea. Beloff's brother-in-law, who now heads the associated Magic Fluke Company, created the designs and crafted the necessary molds in an electric toaster. Most of the work was done by hand. When the prototypes were ready, the Beloffs hit the road.

mahogany FLUKE

What they offered was a line of unique instruments. The quality was and is consistently high and the price consistently moderate. You can buy a Fluke for around $200 and a Flea for somewhat less. Wide choices of models in vivid colors are available, though none of the styles is strictly classic. In their shapes and their shades, both the Fluke and the Flea suggest the exuberance of the Roaring Twenties rather than the restraint of earlier eras.

Another important feature of the line is that these instruments are entirely designed and manufactured on the mainland of the United States. "This is a very big deal for us," Beloff says. The Magic Fluke Company, a separate company led by Beloff's sister Phyllis Webb and her husband Dale Webb, works very closely with Beloff. Dale, who is a gifted engineer, creates the instrument designs and oversees manufacturing. "We call ourselves 'sister' companies," says Beloff.

The Beloffs appear year after year at trade shows and ukulele festivals all over the landscape. They travel up and down the West Coast, to the Midwest, to Hawaii, to New York to Japan, to Australia—wherever the faithful gather and opportunity beckons. In the booths they set up, they demonstrate and display. And up on the stage, they perform. They play together; they sing together. They sell their CDs and DVDs. They make a lot of friends, and have made a respectable amount of change.

To date, Flea Market Music has sold thousands of ukuleles, along with more than 400,000 of Beloff's various books. His Flea Market Music group of artists and authors includes many of the most illustrious citizens of ukeland—Herb Ohta, Lyle Ritz, Fred Sokolow and the late historian and classical ukulele virtuoso, John King. His merchandise offerings continue to grow—T-shirts, ukulele straps, tuners, even ukulele wall hangers and humidifiers. More is sure to come.

Jumpin' Jim's songbooks and Flukes and Fleas can be purchased at retail outfits worldwide, but Beloff's website and mailings produce a good deal of the company's sales. He circulates a regular promotional piece that's part catalogue, part newsletter. It contains

Pineapple Flea

announcements both of new items and forthcoming ukulele events across the country and around the world. One past issue even included a full-page story about a foundation called "Ukuleles for Peace." Its founder, Paul Moore, lives and works in the troubled Middle East, where he brings both Arab and Jewish kids together to play the ukulele and perform. They sing in Hebrew, Arabic and English. The ukulele, it seems, is a citizen of the world.

Beloff is perhaps the ukulele's most dedicated living advocate and ambassador. While he works to preserve its integrity, he also explores its possibilities. He goes on selling. He goes on singing. He goes on smiling.

"Uke can change the world," he says.

And he's not kidding.

hail, hail, the gang's All here

Ukulele Clubs and Congregations

THE UKULELE IS NOT an instrument for solitaries. The guitar is more naturally suited for lonesome broodings. The uke possesses a more convivial gift. It brings people together like the ringing of church bells. Ukulele folks don't merely mingle. They instinctively congregate.

That's why so many ukulele clubs and societies have been generated in recent years. They abound all across the country and around the world. In the United States, many if not most of these fellowships are so small that they don't presume to call themselves clubs at all. They're simply gatherings—people who convene now and then to strum up a storm in somebody's living room. Other groups, though, are bigger and more strictly managed. They schedule regular meetings, elect officers, enact rules, impose membership dues, prepare programs and stage events. Sometimes a ukulele club can become a community asset. They march in parades, perform at graduations and entertain at grand openings.

While the uke may not always be considered a source of serious music, it's generally regarded as a very good citizen.

Of all the clubs in the United States, perhaps the most sizeable and spirited is located about fifty miles south of San Francisco in Santa Cruz, California.

Santa Cruz is a college town. The University of California is its most important industry and chief employer. Many if not most of its 60,000 residents are scholars and students, tolerant in their attitudes and liberal in their opinions. Santa Cruz welcomes people and organizations that march to the beat of different drummers. The town readily adopted the ukulele club as an important member of its civic family.

The group convenes on the third Thursday of every month at a local Italian restaurant called Bocci's Cellar. A stage runs almost the length of one wall. It's furnished at meetings with microphones and other sound equipment.

☛ **The performance stage at DaSilva Ukulele Co. in Berkeley, California, hosts many uke events and concerts.**

A recent gathering began at 6:00 p.m. By 5:30 the room was already beginning to fill up. Many had already opened their ukulele cases and were either tuning up or had started impromptu strum-alongs.

The president of the club, Peter Thomas, is a book artist who's among the country's leading publishers of miniature books. One of his most ambitious works is a set of twenty-five books made out of ukuleles. Each book is nestled inside a genuine uke, is exquisitely illustrated by his wife, is printed on hand-crafted paper, and can be played as well as read. The series took Thomas about five years to complete and the books cost about a thousand dollars apiece. So far, none has been sold, but Thomas is in no hurry to unload them. "These aren't toys or curios," he insists. "I consider them art. In any case, I'm not looking for individual buyers. I'd prefer some museum or library to purchase them as a group. Only an institution, I think, can give them the right kind of care and exposure."

Thomas is in his early fifties. His eyes burn with a brilliant blue intensity, but he's clearly diffident about the authority he yields as president.

"My actual title," he says, "is 'Not Sure Why *I'm* President,'" he says, tongue in cheek. "I was one of the two original founders, but the other guy does just as much work." He pointed across the room. "That's him, Andy Andrews, in the Hawaiian shirt up there on the stage."

Andrews was standing on stage with a group of others, but he clearly seemed the most powerful presence in the group. His shirt implied the force of his personality. Its colors were more strident and its design more aggressive than any in the room. He's cultivated the defiant mustache of a Yugoslav partisan, and he doesn't just smile—he grins. The effect is slightly wolfish. He's officially designated as the club's secretary, but it's not hard to understand why he's sometimes called "our Secretary General."

DEDICATED UKISTS, like old married couples, like to reminisce about how and when they first met and fell in love with their cherished instruments. Neither Thomas nor Andrews was reluctant to describe this ecstatic experience.

"My dad played the uke," Thomas remembered. "Only three chords, but he made them fit any of the old songs we used to sing together. I wasn't much interested in the uke until I went away to college. I was playing bass and guitar in a rock band by then— a *loud* rock band. But one day, at the big flea market we have here in Santa Cruz, I found a neglected old Royal Hawaiian uke. Just the thing, I thought, to play with my dad at family gatherings. It cost me twenty bucks—maybe the best investment I've ever made."

He paused for a moment, thinking back.

"There at the start," he continued, "I played with other people once in awhile. Spur-of-the-moment sessions, you know—just two or three of us, all very spontaneous. Then I began to think about forming a club. I was willing to put in the time, and maybe even to serve as some kind of a leader, but I didn't want to actually run it. I'm better at creating things than I am at managing them. The club needed someone else to act as CEO—someone with exceptional drive and organizational skills." He smiled. "And that's when I met Andy Andrews."

Andrews too related his first encounter with the uke.

"It was over in Hawaii," he said. "I was on the beach one evening, me and my surfboard, watching the sun go down, when I was approached by an old guy who looked like a Hawaiian chieftain out of an MGM movie. 'Do anything else for fun?' he asked me.

"'Not much,' I answered.

"'Better start looking,' he said. 'Find something you can take anywhere and doesn't make you try so hard to stay young. Ever thought about playing the ukulele?'"

Andrews hadn't, but that incident made him consider it. "Wasn't too long," he said, "before I bought myself a nice old Hawaiian uke for $125. There at the beginning, all I played was Hawaiian music. At the same time, I plunged headlong into the Hawaiian way of life. "

Back on the mainland, Andrews began to network with other ukulele enthusiasts. "Peter Thomas was one of those people," Andrews remembered. "He asked me to help him organize a ukulele club here in Santa Cruz, but I hesitated. I'm a very obsessive guy. When I grab hold of a project, I give it everything I've got. It took me awhile to decide if I really wanted to give the uke club that much time and effort. When I finally agreed, it turned out just the way I thought it would. My whole life was ukified."

Together with Peter Thomas, Andrews began to recruit new members and also to search for a permanent place to meet. "I discovered a place that looked ideal. Plenty of space, and the right kind of easy atmosphere. I was a little leery of approaching the owner without some sort of introduction, but as soon as I said 'ukulele' a huge smile spread over his face. 'Brother,' he said, 'you don't have to tell *me*. I was born and raised in Honolulu. That's ukulele heaven.' Ever since then," Andrews concluded, "Bocci's Cellar has been our clubhouse."

The club now has over three hundred members. All this keeps Andrews very busy, and at least once he's been very nearly overwhelmed. That was in 2004, when the club hosted its still celebrated UkeFest West.

"Over seven hundred people showed up," recalled Andrews. "They came from twenty-eight states and five different countries. Some of the best players in the world agreed to perform—and for *free!* Nobody got paid a penny more than their expenses. That took some doing, I can tell you."

Andrews drew a deep breath, as though the memory alone was exhausting.

"Anyway, the whole thing was such a success that we'll probably never do it again. *I* won't, that's for sure. I'll be retired and living in Hawaii. My wife and I bought a piece of jungle over there and have already started construction on our new house. I plan to live pretty much like a native Hawaiian and play the saxophone and also do a lot of painting. I paint landscapes. I love to paint. I *need* to paint. There's more to life than the ukulele, you know."

The club is aware that Andrews intends to move along, and possible successors are already being discussed. Andrews himself declines to be involved in the choice. "Don't even think about it much," he said. "One way or another, the club will find its own way. It's not my property. It's not *anybody's* property. It may take off in an entirely different direction—perhaps even split up into different groups. Who knows?" Under his fierce mustache, his teeth flashed. "Over in the islands I'm going to be obsessed by very different things."

BEVERLY WESLEY and Georgene Goodwin, who form a team called the Broken G Strings, testify their allegiance to the club through regular and very popular appearances both at club meetings and elsewhere throughout the Santa Cruz area.

The two of them have been friends and partners for over thirty years. Both were once "Sweet Adelines," the celebrated women's barbershop chorus. Both were teachers at the same Santa Cruz school. And both played the banjo.

"We got started by doing our thing at faculty functions," Bev told me. "Stunts, antics, nonsense stuff. We dressed up in outlandish costumes. We also worked weddings, private parties, retirement homes—whatever came along."

the broken g strings

"But those banjos wore us out," Georgene said. That began a verbal duet.

Bev: "They were heavy."

Georgene: "Too heavy."

Bev: "All that sharp metal."

Georgene: "They could bruise you. They could cut you."

Bev: "They *did* bruise and cut us."

Georgene: "Goodbye, banjos. Hello ukes!"

Their shift from banjos to ukes occurred some years ago, when Bev noticed an ad in the local newspaper. It was an attempt to recruit new members for the Santa Cruz Ukulele Club. "Andy Andrews had persuaded the editor to run it as a favor," Bev recalled. "I attended the next meeting, just to investigate. One visit and I was hooked. I went right out and bought a uke for myself."

"Me, too," Georgene said. "It was love at first strum."

"The Broken G Strings" makes it sound as though their material is lurid, but Bev vehemently denies it. "Don't you believe it," she protested. "Unusual, maybe, but nothing that wouldn't get the Good Housekeeping Seal of Approval."

As evidence, she cited a few of the team's most eccentric numbers:

"Frog Kissin'"

"Please, Mr. Columbus (Won't You Turn This Ship Around?)"

"Washington at Valley Forge"

"Runaround Sue"

"Twenty-Six Miles Across the Sea"

The G Strings have excavated their repertoire from many different sources, but chiefly from the musty sheet music of the 1920s and '30s. Many of their numbers have been nearly forgotten, if in fact they were ever really remembered. As often as not, their audiences don't know the relics that the G Strings have retrieved from the past.

"We're rehearsing a new piece right now," Bev added. "We plan to play it at the club's next open-mic session. It's a novelty number called 'How Can I Miss You if You Won't Go Away?' Ever heard that one?"

She asked the question, but it's pretty sure she already knew the answer.

celina gutierrez

CELINA GUTIERREZ, a short compact woman in her mid-thirties, possesses a smile that might make the uke itself break out smiling.

She smiled more or less constantly as she described how the uke first seduced her. That was in 1991, when she went to Hawaii shortly after a long and intense romance foundered and failed. "It wasn't a vacation," she said. "I was devastated. I was hoping for some kind of renewal—even a transformation. Believe it or not, something of the sort actually happened. And on top of that"—here she quoted the title of a song that was a hit back in the Roaring Twenties—"'I Found a New Baby.'"

Her new baby wasn't any noble Hawaiian warrior, she explained—nothing like that. It was a ukulele. Not a distinguished uke, either, just an unexceptional specimen that she picked up for $100. "I've since learned that I might have paid too much," she said. "But I don't care. For me it was a real bargain. That uke helped me change my life."

Celina was no musical novice. She'd been playing the guitar since she was ten years old. During her twenties, she sang and played guitar with many different groups in several different styles. "Everything from mariachi bands to rock-and-roll," she said. "But when I moved to Santa Cruz in 1997, things changed. Between my job and my love affair, there wasn't much room left for performing. The practicing, the rehearsals, the gigs themselves—all that takes a lot of time and energy. So I more or less dropped out of music, at least as a professional."

When she returned from Hawaii to Santa Cruz, Celina immediately sat down with her new uke to master its rudiments. Right from the first chord she felt a special relationship with the ukulele. As soon as she'd tutored herself in the basics, Celina joined the Santa Cruz Ukulele Club. "I'd already heard about it, of course," she said. "Everybody around here seems to know about the club, even if they don't care very much about the uke. It's

become kind of an institution around here. But nothing I'd been told really prepared me for what I experienced."

That smile of hers spread across her broad face.

"I needed support at that time," she continued. "And believe me, I *got* support. It was incredible. When I got up there on the stage for the first time I received the obligatory standing ovation. But it was more than applause. It was a wave of acceptance. It went on and on, like the tide, like the surf. I still feel it, whether I'm playing or whether I'm not. I don't think it will ever stop."

She picked up her ukulele and tenderly brushed her fingers across the strings. "I wonder," she said, "why some people need a strap to support so small and fragile an instrument. Do you need a strap to help you cuddle a baby?" She brushed the strings again. "I hold my uke the way I'd hold a child," she said. "Next to my heart."

AFTER THE HOUSE BAND had kicked off the meeting with a few time-honored numbers, Andy Andrews signaled them to stop. Then he stepped forward and took over the microphone.

"We seem to have quite a few newcomers tonight," he said, "so maybe I'd better explain how things work around here. We're a rather

the
UKULELE
CLUB OF
SANta CRUZ

relaxed bunch. No rules, no dues. If you want to join us, just show up. Your second visit automatically makes you a member."

Andrews shifted his stance and also his tone. "I just said that we have no rules in this club. But we *do* have some traditions. One is that anyone who performs on our stage for the first time gets a standing ovation. Got that? A guaranteed standing O. A second tradition is what we're going to do now—play 'Under the Boardwalk,' our theme song. To do that, you may need our official songbook"—he held it up—"which contains the words and chord diagrams. And if you require any further help, it's waiting in the wings. Come on, people. Let's hear it for"—Andrews began to clap—"the Chordettes."

There was an immediate volley of applause. Four middle-aged women got to their feet and proceeded to the stage. All of them carried a placard about three feet square. Printed on each was a particular chord symbol—C, F, G and so on—together with a simple diagram of how that chord should be played—one at a time.

"We're in the friendly key of C," Andrews proclaimed. One of the Chordettes lifted the appropriate card high above her head. Andrews counted out the tempo—"one, two, three, four—and about 150 ukuleles lurched into simultaneous action. The group went right on strumming, right on singing, right on struggling, all the way through to the untidy finish.

This was one of the club's "open-mic" nights. Only club members were permitted to perform. A couple were experts. Others simply did the best they could. Everybody got about the same enthusiastic helping of applause.

A trio—bass, ukulele, and a man who tinkled partly filled water glasses with a spoon—contributed a couple of songs that earned a polite response.

A woman in a muumuu and adorned with flowers in her hair sang a song she'd learned as a girl in the islands. The lyrics were naughty, she warned. "But I'm doing them in Hawaiian," she added, "so the younger generation won't get bad habits."

When at last no other members were listed to perform, Andy Andrews invited volunteers. "Anybody else?" he exhorted. "Who else has something to offer?"

All this time, a pale and very thin girl of about eight had been inching closer and closer to the stage. An older woman leaned forward and said in a half whisper, "Would you like to get up there, honey? Would you like to sing a song?"

The girl hesitated for a long moment, and then nodded yes. The older woman gently took the girl by the hand and led her up the steps and into the spotlight. She struck an introductory chord on her uke. "What do you want to sing?" she asked.

The girl answered with the title of the song that's more frequently requested of ukulele players than any other ever written. "You Are My Sunshine," she said.

She sang it all the way through in a small, shy voice, never forgetting a word or drifting off key. As she finished, the whole room surged to its feet. The applause went on and on—a standing O. The little girl stood there, transfixed with pure pleasure, as the cheers continued to embrace her.

There was a message in that ovation.

"Welcome to the club," it seemed to say. "Welcome to the club."

refrain

I SAID at the beginning of this book that it was intended to be an entertainment, not an opus.

Now that we're coming to the end of it, I feel that I've delivered on that promise.

The story I've tried to tell is nowhere near complete. Omissions abound, and most of them have been deliberate. In general, I've concentrated on the events and personalities that really interest me and sidestepped the lackluster material that doesn't. In other words, I've written a book that I myself might like to read. If a more solemn and professorial treatment of the subject is required, some other author will have to do the heavy lifting.

Because this doesn't presume to be a work of scholarship, you may observe that it lacks the customary reference supports. No bibliography. No glossary. No footnotes—in fact, no notes at all.

Now, I don't mean to suggest that what I've produced is simply a piece of fluff. There's some nourishment to be found in the preceding pages—some surprises, some amusement, some controversy, some tragedy, some exhilarating successes. In any case, one thing is certain. I, the writer, learned a whole lot while the book was taking shape. The experience became an education.

Of all the enlightenments I received, one in particular glows with significance. Right from the start of my research, the enthusiasts I interviewed began to suggest that the ukulele possessed some special and very potent spiritual powers. These statements were repeated again and again, by all kinds of people, at many different times and in many different places. It surfaces now and then throughout the book—a recurring refrain, a collective murmur. Sometimes the statement is oblique, sometimes direct. But it rises to the surface as insistently as the bubbles in a glass of champagne and sometimes produces the same giddy effect.

To repeat certain of the remarks already quoted in the text, here are just some of the things I was told.

"Anyone who plays the ukulele can't be all bad."

"It's the ukulele that brings us together."

"I hold my ukulele the way I'd hold a child—close to my heart."

"We don't just belong to a ukulele club. We belong to a congregation."

"The ukulele just makes people smile."

"You can't play the blues on a ukulele."

I couldn't ignore those messages. They were too consistently and passionately expressed. The messengers truly believe that Adolph Hitler could never, never, ever have played the ukulele. They believe that they and their ukes form some kind of a brotherhood. They believe their club meetings are held in a restaurant that, on the third Thursday of every month, becomes a sort of church. "Uke can change the world," is Jim Beloff's slogan for Flea Market Music, and Beloff's purpose is not just to move merchandise. Jim really means it.

So far as I know, this is an attribute of the ukulele that's never been discussed in depth or in detail. I've found no mention of it in print. Nobody speaks of it as a prevailing attitude or as an article of faith.

But the writing of this book has converted me. Now I too believe that the belief is real, that the believers are true believers, and that their testimony can be trusted.

"Anyone who plays the ukulele can't be all bad."

Do you believe it too?

resources

Clubs

Berkeley Ukulele Club
 Mike DaSilva
 510-649-1548
 www.ukemaker.com/ukeclub/

www.curtsheller.com/ukulele/clubs/
 A listing of ukulele clubs in the U.S. and around the world, and information about starting a club

Monterey Ukulele Club
 Steve and Barbara Brooks
 steve27@pacbell.net
 831-624-7022

Santa Cruz Ukulele Club
 ukuleleclub.com

General Information

Ukulele Guild of Hawaii
 www.ukuleleguild.org
 History of the ukulele, lessons and tablatures, events

The Ukulele Hall of Fame Museum
 www.ukulele.org
 Biographies of ukulele musicians, history of the ukulele

Ukulele Hunt
 ukulelehunt.com
 Lessons, tabs and chords, information about buying instruments

Ukulele Underground
 www.ukuleleunderground.com
 Ukulele videos, lessons, online groups and forums

Manufacturers and Retailers

DaSilva Ukulele Co.
 2547 8th Street, Suite 28
 Berkeley, CA 94710
 510-649-1548
 www.ukemaker.com
 Handcrafted ukuleles

Flea Market Music
 www.fleamarketmusic.com
 info@fleamarketmusic.com
 Instruments, songbooks, CDs, accessories, and more

Kamaka Hawaii, Inc.
 550 South Street
 Honolulu, HI 96813
 808-531-3165
 www.kamakahawaii.com

Martin Guitar Co.
 510 Sycamore Street
 Nazareth, PA 18064
 610-759-2837
 martinguitar.com

Ukulele 101

Today, most players use C tuning. In this tuning, the individual strings from the top (closest to your nose) to bottom (closest to your toes) are tuned GCEA. A lot of the most commonly used chords can be made with one or two fingers, and many simple songs can be played with four chords or less.

Uke C Tuning

One easy way to tune a ukulele is with a pitchpipe or electronic tuner matching the strings with the notes.

This corresponds to that famous melody:

Here are the notes on the piano:

My dog has fleas

Keeping In Tune

Most ukuleles have friction tuners that include a small screw at the end of the tuner. The secret to staying in tune is to keep these screws tight enough so that the tuners don't slip, but loose enough that the tuners still turn.

Holding The Uke

Press your uke against your body about two-thirds of the way up your forearm. Your strumming hand should naturally fall on top of the upper frets (not over the soundhole). Hold the neck of the uke between your thumb and first finger of your other hand, so that your fingers are free to move about the fretboard.

Note: See *Jumpin' Jim's Ukulele Tips 'N' Tunes* if you need a basic ukulele method book.

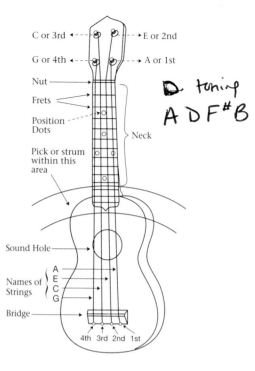

D. tuning
A D F#B

These pages adapted from excerpts from *The Daily Ukulele* (HL#240356). Flea Market Music publications are available at book and music stores nationwide or through www.fleamarketmusic.com.
The Daily Ukulele
Compiled and arranged by Liz and Jim Beloff
© 2010 Flea Market Music, Inc.

140

Making The Chords

You make chords by putting various combinations of fingers on the fretboard. Typically in ukulele songbooks you'll find chord diagrams that show where to put your fingers to make the right sound. The vertical lines in the diagrams represent strings and the horizontal lines represent the frets. The numbers at the bottom of the chords shown here indicate what fingers to use.

1 = Index finger
2 = Second finger
3 = Ring finger
4 = Pinky

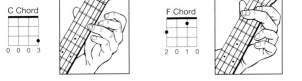

C Chord
0 0 0 3

F Chord
2 0 1 0

G7 Chord
0 2 1 3

Remember to:

1. When pressing down the strings, use the tips of your fingers.
2. Always press down in the space between the frets, not on them.
3. Press the strings down to the fingerboard. If you hear a buzz it may be because you are not pressing hard enough or are too close to a fret.
4. Keep your thumb at the back of the neck, parallel to the frets.

Making The Strums

The Common Strum: This is the most basic up/down strum. It can be produced solely with your index finger going down the strings with the fingernail and up with the cushion of your fingertip. You can also try this with the pad of your thumb running down the strings and the tip of your index finger going up. This strum works fine for many songs.

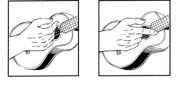

Waltz Strum: This ¾ rhythm can be produced simply with your thumb or index finger in sets of three down strums. You can use this on ¾ songs.

Island Strum: This lilting, syncopated strum is a combination of quick up and down strums plus a roll. In a typical 4-beat measure it would look like this:

⊓ = downstroke

∨ = upstroke

⊓   roll ∨   ∨ ⊓ ∨

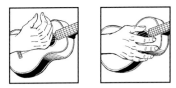

Here's how to make the roll strum.

One and **Two** and **Three** and **Four** and…

Play the downstroke with your thumb and the upstroke with your index finger. The roll is made by running the ring, middle and index fingers quickly in succession across the strings.

Tremolo: This is used often as an ending flourish for a song. It's produced by running your index finger across the strings rapidly. If you are performing, this will suggest to your audience that you are finishing the song and they should get ready to applaud. Try this at the end of any song where you want a "big finish."

Ukulele Chords

G = G, C, D
C = C, F, G

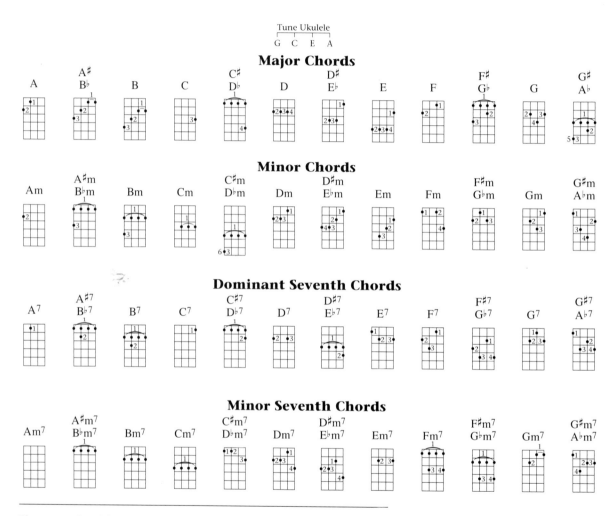

These pages adapted from excerpts from *The Daily Ukulele* (HL#240356). Flea Market Music publications are available at book and music stores nationwide or through www.fleamarketmusic.com.
The Daily Ukulele
Compiled and arranged by Liz and Jim Beloff
© 2010 Flea Market Music, Inc.
All rights reserved

Major Sixth Chords

A⁶   A♯6 B♭6   B⁶   C⁶   C♯6 D♭6   D⁶   D♯6 E♭6   E⁶   F⁶   F♯6 G♭6   G⁶   G♯6 A♭6

Minor Sixth Chords

Am⁶   A♯m6 B♭m6   Bm⁶   Cm⁶   C♯m6 D♭m6   Dm⁶   D♯m6 E♭m6   Em⁶   Fm⁶   F♯m6 G♭m6   Gm⁶   G♯m6 A♭m6

Major Seventh Chords

Amaj⁷   A♯maj7 B♭maj7   Bmaj⁷   Cmaj⁷   C♯maj7 D♭maj7   Dmaj⁷   D♯maj7 E♭maj7   Emaj⁷   Fmaj⁷   F♯maj7 G♭maj7   Gmaj⁷   G♯maj7 A♭maj7

Augmented Fifth Chords (+ or aug)

A+   A♯+ B♭+   B+   C+   C♯+ D♭+   D+   D♯+ E♭+   E+   F+   F♯+ G♭+   G+   G♯+ A♭+

Diminished Seventh Chords (dim)

Adim   A♯dim B♭dim   Bdim   Cdim   C♯dim D♭dim   Ddim   D♯dim E♭dim   Edim   Fdim   F♯dim G♭dim   Gdim   G♯dim A♭dim

photo credits

Courtesy Beverly Wesley and
Georgene Goodwin
134

Courtesy C. F. Martin Archives
60–61

Courtesy Celina Gutierrez
135

Courtesy Kamaka Hawaii, Inc.
66, 67, 68, 103–105

Ila Desai, courtesy Amanda Palmer
99 (bottom)

Dixie Dixon
6, 8–9 (ukulele), 10, 20–21,
22–23, 31, 59, 62 (bottom), 100,
101, 107–115, 119, 120, 121
(right), 123, 131, 132

iofoto / shutterstock.com
Blue painted ukulele used
throughout

J. Gracey Stinson
1

Kelly Hironaka / shutterstock.com
All floral patterns and floral
graphics used throughout

Image Makers, courtesy Langley
Ukulele Ensemble
97

Aaron Kotowski, courtesy Flea
Market Music, Inc.
127

Elizabeth Maihock Beloff, courtesy
Flea Market Music, Inc.
128, 129

MPTV Images (mptvimages.com)
73, 75

Sandor Nagyszalanczy
4–5, 11, 14 (sheet music), 16–17
(ukulele), 18, 24 (ukulele),
25–27, 29, 30, 32–42, 46–48,
51, 52 (ukulele), 56–58, 62–63,
64–65, 70, 71, 74, 81, 121 (left)

Rick Scanlan, courtesy Flea Market
Music, Inc.
124

Stephen Wright / shutterstock.com
8 (map), 14 (map)